D1257131

LANDSCAPE DESIGN DOCUMENTATION

LANDSCAPE DESIGN DOCUMENTATION

STRATEGIES FOR PLAN CHECKING AND QUALITY CONTROL

BRIAN THOMAS McDONALD

WILEY

John Wiley & Sons, Inc.

Library of Congress Cataloging-in-Publication Data:

McDonald, Brian Thomas.
  Landscape design documentation : a guide to plan checking and quality
control / by Brian Thomas McDonald.
     p. cm.
  Includes bibliographical references and index.
ISBN 13: 0-978-0471-76137-2 (Cloth)
ISBN 10: 0-471-76137-0 (Cloth)
  1. Landscape design—Quality control.   I. Title.
  SB472.45M39 2006
  712′.3—dc22

                                                    2005028990

Printed in the United States of America

10 9 8 7 6 5 4 3 2 1

To Jocelyn, Guinevere, and Samantha

CONTENTS

PREFACE

Many good books have been written on implementing quality control measures for architecture and engineering firms; however, this book applies specifically to landscape architecture. The purpose of this book is to identify the typical scope of services provided by landscape architects; identify common risk exposures and how to manage those risks; identify the components of a quality control plan; and provide checklist tables as a guide to plan checking.

Landscape architecture firms can use these documents and checklist tables to establish or complement an existing quality control plan. They can benefit from the information provided to ensure all critical items during the plan checking process have been reviewed. Project managers can use this as a guide to improve the quality of drawings and to educate staff about what is to be included on drawings.

This book will be useful in educating students in professional practice, design, and construction courses. Key issues to educate students involve information to be included on drawings and how a project is sequenced through an office. Related disciplines can use this book to develop familiarity with the scope and services of landscape architects. Many federal, state, and city agencies that utilize services or approve plans submitted by landscape architects will find the checklists useful in reviewing these drawings. The book can also help clients gain insight into the scope of work and responsibilities of the landscape architect.

Part I defines landscape architecture, outlines the ethical and legal aspects of the profession, and discusses the expanding role and diverse types of projects involved. Additional topics are typical project services, description of phases of work, business structure, and collaboration with other professionals.

Part II highlights the most common risk exposures facing landscape architects during different phases of work, and includes measures to take in order to minimize these risks. Case studies are provided as examples. Identification is made of risk management techniques through insurance in order to protect the business, employees, and subcontracted work. Methods of resolving disputes are indicated, highlighting the pros and cons of each procedure.

Part III defines the five essential components of a quality control plan. Quality control procedures and processes for plan checking include instructions for the application of the checklist tables in Part IV. Plan checking and risk management specific to CAD drawings are also discussed.

Part IV provides checklist tables for information to be gathered from the beginning to the end of projects. Tables encompass data collection, consultant coordination, design documentation, construction documents, specifications, cost estimating, bidding, site observation, and project closeout.

The contents of this book are complete and comprehensive. No materials contained herein, however, are intended to replace or supersede federal, state, or local laws, construction codes, or legal standards.

ACKNOWLEDGMENTS

For my continuing education, I wish to thank all the teachers, mentors, and colleagues I have had the honor to associate with in the past and present. I am also grateful to the companies, coworkers, and other professionals whose collaboration has contributed to my continual quest for knowledge. But most of all, I am indebted to my family, whose time I have exploited in order to compile and compose this information.

I would like to thank certain individuals for their participation in interviews and reviews used in this book. Mr. Jim Leatzow, for his input regarding professional liability insurance; Mr. Steve Sharafian, for his knowledge regarding dispute resolution; Mr. Clark Cowley and Mr. Hunter McLean, for their review of legal matters; Mr. Chris Hollmann, for his review of insurance matters; and Mr. Chris Schexnayder and Mr. Blair Baker, both members of the Texas Registered Accessibility Specialists Association, for their review of the ADA Accessibility Requirements Checklist. I would also like to thank Mr. William Bibb, Mr. Thomas Pritchett, Mr. Timothy May, and Mr. David Hopman, who gave time for interviews.

Last, but not least, I would like to thank Mrs. Margaret Cummins and her team at John Wiley & Sons for their continued support and guidance throughout the publishing process.

PART I

ROLE OF THE LANDSCAPE ARCHITECT

CHAPTER 1

Definition and Practice

DEFINITION

The role of the landscape architect is expanding and specializing, no more so than in the last two decades. What started formally as a profession in 1899 with the establishment of the American Society of Landscape Architects (ASLA) landscape architecture has developed into a multifaceted profession, with projects ranging from small, intimate gardens to urban and regional town planning and everything in between. With increasing concern over environmental issues and the quality of design, the landscape architect is being employed by residential and commercial clients as well as federal and state agencies.

To define the role of landscape architects we look to ASLA, the professional organization, for the ethics and guidelines governing the practice, including:

- Mission, Goals, and Objectives
- ASLA Code of Professional Ethics
- ASLA Constitution
- ASLA Bylaws

These can be found online at http://www.asla.org or by writing to the organization at:

American Society of Landscape Architects
636 Eye Street NW
Washington, DC 20001-3736

The ASLA's broad definition of landscape architecture is "the art and science of analysis, planning, design, management, preservation and rehabilitation of the land."[1] State regulating boards also provide detailed definitions under the rules and regulations governing the practice in their state. These are legal descriptions of how the landscape architect is to serve and perform.

Due to the vast scope and services of the profession it is difficult to develop a concise definition to landscape architecture. Education and practice involve an overlapping knowledge of art, botany, ecology, geography, geology, horticulture, agriculture, architecture, business, graphic design, and civil engineering.

What is landscape architecture to the general public?

The primary objective of landscape architecture is to protect the health, safety, and welfare of the public. Few people, however, are familiar with what a landscape architect does or how the profession affects them, and they do not know what the practice involves. This may be due to marketing or perhaps terminology. People hear the word *landscape* and immediately think about contracting, gardening, or horticulture.

"As the public becomes more aware of conservation, mitigation, environmental impacts, and recreational needs, the profession of landscape architecture will be recognized as an important element in today's society."

Timothy May, ASLA

Landscape architects are needed to provide competence in design and implementation of projects utilized by both public and private benefactors. Regulation of the profession establishes a minimum competency level, reduces negligence, and limits defective design. Licensure acts (in effect in 47 of 50 states as of 2005) give the landscape architect the right to practice in the state where the national exam was passed.

Many cities and agencies require certified plans and specifications prepared by landscape architects prior to development approvals and permits. Using certified professionals gives agencies the security of knowing the plans will meet minimum standards; approvals are thus expedited.

Where no landscape architecture licensure act is in force, a gray area emerges between architecture and engineering. The following case study shows how a landscape architect's expertise could have prevented inadequacies in design.

CASE STUDY 1-1   Poor School Design in Western Colorado

In 1990, a school district was having significant structural problems in two of its buildings. At School A, water was leaking through walls with obvious damage to floors, finishes, and so on. At School B, an entire wing of the building had shifted significantly to the point where the flat roof no longer pitched in the correct direction. The school district blamed the building architects; the architects claimed overwatering practices by the school maintenance staff caused the problems. The building architects had employed a landscape architect for planting design on School A but not School B, and neither school's architects used a landscape architect for irrigation design.

An expert witness for the case, Ted Ciavonne, was able to show that the problems at the two schools were similar: (1) poor grading/negative grading around the buildings; (2) poor irrigation design (mixing hot and cold spots, significantly different precipitation rates within individual zones, low head drainage); and (3) poor plant selection (mixing high and low water users). When any of these issues occurred together, the problems were compounded. School maintenance had applied programmed quantities of water over entire school sites, but within each site this resulted in the application of too much or too little water due to the inadequate design.

At both schools, Mr.Ciavonne's firm made design recommendations/corrections for grading, paving (creation of concrete plazas where grades were too flat to irrigate and drain), landscape, and irrigation. The firm determined that at School A, the architects had done a poor job with site grading and had left the landscape and irrigation design for a design-build approach. The design-build contractor made many technical mistakes, but from the court's standpoint the overall responsibility fell to the building architects. School B was much more interesting. When the building architect's subconsultant landscape architect reviewed the firm's comments, criticisms, and design solutions, the landscape architect informed Mr. Ciavonne that the original plans had design solutions similar to those now being recommended. He had old correspondence to his prime consultant (the building architect) warning of the potential for the grading problems now in evidence. For unknown reasons, the building architect had eliminated plazas and shrub planting areas from the landscape architect's plans without his permission.

Impact

This case shows the lasting impact of landscape architecture on the community's health, safety, and welfare. The other design professionals did not adhere to the landscape architect's plans. As a result, not only did the plantings suffer but so did the structural integrity of the buildings, and perhaps the children themselves also suffered.

Further, the publicly funded school district experienced financial harm. The district ended up paying much more than if the original design of the landscape architect had been implemented in the first place. The damage could have resulted in physical harm to students as a result of the poor irrigation and pooling of water. Additionally, the school district could have suffered losses from the lost use of the facilities if the problem had been allowed to proceed unchecked much longer.

Source: Mr. Ted Ciavonne, owner of Ciavonne & Associates, Inc., a landscape architecture and planning firm in Grand Junction, Colorado, was an expert witness for these cases in western Colorado.[2]

BECOMING A LANDSCAPE ARCHITECT

Certain education and experience requirements must be fulfilled before taking the Landscape Architecture Registration Exam (LARE). Once the LARE is passed, the landscape architect is licensed to practice in the state in which it was taken. Some states require continuing education courses as a prerequisite for renewal of licensure.

The minimum education requirement to become a landscape architect is a BLA, BSLA, or MLA degree from an accredited university. A core curriculum of classes typically consists of landscape design, landscape construction, grading and drainage, plant material, professional practice, communication skills, and history and theory. Other courses may include ecology, soil science, geology, agriculture, and horticulture. Each school requires a specific number of hours in order to obtain the degree.

Experience requirements may call for recent graduates to work under the supervision of a registered landscape architect for a specified period in order to gain experience and develop knowledge and skills in the profession. This can take place in either the public or private sector.

Once education and experience requirements are fulfilled, the next step is to take the LARE. The LARE is prepared and administered by the Council of Landscape Architectural Boards (CLARB), an independent, nonprofit organization. The LARE is held on an annual basis, and as of 2005 includes five test sections, namely:

- Legal and Administrative Aspects of Practice
- Analytical Aspects of Practice
- Planning and Site Design
- Structural Considerations and Materials and Methods of Construction
- Grading, Drainage, and Stormwater Management

Passing each section of the exam allows the individual to obtain licensure in the state where it was administered. Each state has a board that develops and enforces regulations governing the practice of landscape architecture. These state boards frequently work together with similar professions such as architecture, engineering, and interior design. Some states have reciprocity laws that grant licenses to landscape architects from other states. In some cases, provisions allow for short-term licenses to be granted in connection with a specific project.

Although the LARE is a standard national exam, registration is administered by individual states due to differences in climate, geology, construction methods, and governing laws. The following two case studies are prime examples of the importance of specific state licensure.

CASE STUDY 1-2   Site Planning

Especially in dry climates and densely forested regions, competent landscape architects incorporate design techniques to mitigate significant fire hazards. These techniques, known generally as *defensible space,* have been credited with saving homes in recent Western wildfires.[3]

As demonstrated by the lack of property damage experienced directly in the path of recent blazes, effective defensible space techniques including selective tree-thinning, strategic siting of structures, driveway alignment as a firebreak, and strategic irrigation.

In one California case where defensible space techniques were largely absent, close proximity of vegetation to power lines and houses ignited a 25,000-acre wildfire and caused at least $2.2 million in property damage.[4]

CASE STUDY 1-3 Skatepark Design Ignores Local Conditions

The town of Crested Butte, Colorado, hired a company from Florida to design and build a public skatepark on town property. The company constructed the park of cast-in-place concrete with swimming pool coping. This company was not aware of the typical freeze/thaw cycles of the Colorado climate and installed an inappropriate material at the edge of a 10-foot-deep bowl. Moisture seeped through the joints, froze, and heaved the pool coping off, leading to a hazardous and unsafe condition in the public skatepark. While we are unaware of any lawsuits, discussions with local skaters have turned up severe injuries requiring hospital visits.

Impact

This case resulted in financial harm to the Town of Crested Butte for increased regular maintenance costs to fix the initial faulty design. Licensed landscape architects are trained in local climate conditions and take these variables into account when producing project designs. In this case, the lack of experience with local freeze/thaw cycles created hazardous conditions. The poor design led to a tangible threat to public safety, resulting in physical harm to several.

Source: From the application to the Colorado Department of Regulatory Agencies for regulation and licensure of the profession of landscape architecture (July 1, 2001).[5]

Some states have a prerequisite for renewal of licensure through required continuing education credit hours. Education courses are offered through ASLA, annual state chapter meetings, university programs, and online seminars. Some states also require a certain number of hours in specific areas such as barrier-free design.

What led you to become a landscape architect, and how did you find out about the profession?

I had the opportunity to interview a number of landscape architects in both the private and academic sectors in order to find out how they became involved in the profession. A general trend involved many having an interest in the outdoors and a general concern with environmental issues. They were well traveled and had a keen perception of ecology and ecosystems of different places. They were able to visually read the character of the land. Art, architecture, and drafting skills were also predominant interests. Many started in architecture programs at the university level, where they then discovered the existence of landscape architecture, urban design, and city and regional planning. In my case, a blending of architecture, a concern for the environment, and a strong landscape architect mentor were the natural lead-ins to my career.

ETHICAL RESPONSIBILITIES

In 1899, the American Society of Landscape Architects (ASLA) was founded. The ASLA organized and defined the profession, established a code of ethics, and set goals and objectives for professional practice. As of 2005, forty-seven states license the practice of landscape architecture, and ASLA has over 15,000 members in forty-eight chapters.[6]

The ASLA Code of Professional Ethics is built on "protecting the health, safety and welfare of the public and recognition and protection of the land and its resources."[7] These ethics are established to safeguard the client, the public, and the landscape architect. The landscape architect is obliged to conform to the ethical code, which describes the requirements of responsibility for acceptable practice. The code of ethics also provides standards for competence, resume preparation, sealing of documents, and pro bono services.

Competence is having the knowledge, skills, and abilities to perform the minimum standard of care in the profession. When soliciting work, the landscape architect should advertise only the project types and services in which they are competent, experienced, and trained. Brochures and other marketing materials may not overstate qualifications or services, nor may they mislead the audience about the landscape architect's experience in any specialty area.

CASE STUDY 1-4 Skatepark Design Review Proves Invaluable

The town of Parker, Colorado, hired an inexperienced landscape architect to design a public skatepark in a regional park. This individual worked with the local skating community and developed a design plan for the skatepark. The town asked a second landscape architect, who was licensed in another state, to review the plan prior to putting it out for bids from contractors. The licensed landscape architect found the following flaws in the plan:

- The skatepark encroached across park property onto private property.
- The proposed grading plan included a significant amount of fill in the Cherry Creek floodplain.
- The skatepark included proposed cuts and fills over an existing sanitary sewer line and easement.
- The proposed main entry was to be located immediately adjacent to a regional bicycle trail, which would invite user conflicts and potentially serious injuries.

Impact

The flaws in the original plan could have had significant effects on the public through direct physical harm and environmental impact as well as indirect financial harm through costs incurred by the city. The conflict between the main entry and the adjacent properties was clearly a safety issue with the potential to create collisions and physical injuries. The grading plan would have had a negative environmental impact. If damage had been done to the sewer lines, both environmental and financial costs would have been incurred. Perhaps most significantly, the town would have been at risk for numerous liabilities, including property rights and safety issues. This case resulted in financial harm to the town, which paid an inexperienced individual to perform professional services and then was required to pay a licensed landscape architect to revise the plan and proceed with the project.

Source: From the application to the Colorado Department of Regulatory Agencies for regulation and licensure of the profession of landscape architecture (July 1, 2001).[8]

As in advertising, professional resumes should reflect only those project types with which the landscape architect has experience. Work done under the employment of others must be indicated as such, with the design firm of record given the appropriate credit.

Sealing documents is required by states that regulate the practice of landscape architecture. Sealed documents are generally required for regulatory approval, permitting, and construction purposes. The appropriate drawings and documents must be sealed, signed, and dated, and the seal should be used to certify the work only when:

- The documents are prepared under the direct supervision of the landscape architect whose seal is affixed to the drawings.
- The landscape architect is qualified and competent to do the work being sealed.
- When the drawing includes work done by others, the exact extent of that work must be noted as such prior to sealing.

If the landscape architect is sealing work, such as certifying the work of an out-of-state landscape architect, the governing landscape architect must perform the following prior to sealing the drawings:

- The licensee must review the work to confirm that it will meet with the codes and laws of that state. Any nonconformance must be brought to the attention of the client and original design professional in writing prior to modifications being done.
- The names of both the licensee and other design professionals must appear on the drawings.
- Any modifications to the original design professional's work must be clearly noted on the drawings.
- If the original design professional was terminated, the client must verify the copyright to the design. The client must provide a statement to the new landscape architect that he or she has the copyright to the original design professional's drawings.

For pro bono work, the landscape architect should adhere to the same regulations and laws governing the practice. It is still essential to have a signed contract that clearly defines the scope of services. The work should be performed in the same manner and to the same standard of care as a paid contract.

LEGAL RESPONSIBILITIES

A landscape architect is an individual who holds a valid registration certification granted by the state in which he or she practices. The permission to practice is obtained by completing education and experience requirements and by passing the LARE. Once registered, the landscape architect must abide by the rules and regulations of the state board. Failure to do so can result in reprimands, penalties, suspension, or revocation of license to practice.

The landscape architect is responsible for carrying out the terms of the contract with the client and for working with the contractor to properly administer the construction contract. Further, he or she is responsible to the general public as well as employees for their health, safety, and welfare.

PROFESSIONAL LIABILITY

Liability concerns that may affect the landscape architect include the following:

- Common-law torts including negligence, negligence per se, and fraud
- Breach of contract
- Conveying wrong information provided by others
- Liability to third parties

Additional bases for liability also exist; however, the purpose here is to highlight the most frequent concerns. The information provided here is not intended to be legal advice. All legal matters should be addressed by a reputable licensed attorney.

Tort Liability

Tort liability is generally defined as a civil wrongdoing that gives rise to a claim pursuant to the common law even in the absence of a contract or statue. The most common tort claim asserted against landscape architects is negligence. Fraud can also be claimed.

Because landscape architects are licensed professionals, they are held to a certain standard of care in the performance of their services. Negligence occurs when a duty is owed from one person to another, which duty is breached, and which breach causes harm. The applicable standard of care defines the duties owed. Negligence can occur due to an infraction by accident or by performance not meeting a normal standard of care. Negligence and malpractice are unintentional torts. Negligence per se is a violation of a code, statute, or ordinance that establishes the applicable duty or standard of care.

Negligence can occur in connection with the performance of duties relating to design, construction drawings, specifications, or site observation. Negligence occurring during the design stage is usually due to incomplete site inventory or analysis. It may also be due to lack of familiarity with local codes, guidelines, or ordinances. Cities and subdivisions also have codes that affect the design of projects.

Negligence found in construction drawings and specifications is commonly due to error and omission. Landscape architects, therefore, should not seal or issue construction drawings until the plans are thoroughly reviewed and checked. Errors and omissions on construction drawings can have a great impact on the bid pricing, construction schedules, or structural integrity of the project. Contractors can also claim economic loss due to negligence in the preparation of plans. Landscape architecture firms typically employ a key staff member with many years of experience who checks and corrects the drawings before they are issued outside of the office.

Construction observation is another phase of work where negligence may occur. The landscape architect is liable for site decisions or recommendations to the contractor, either through field orders, or change orders, where cost and time are major factors. Careful attention to material samples, substitutions, shop drawings, certifications of progress claims, and substantial and final completion approvals are all critical elements during this phase of work. Once the project is completed a Statute of Limitations (Statute of Repose) comes into effect. The time period differs depending upon state laws. This statute applies only to property damage and not for personal injury cases.

The standard of care is how landscape architects must act and carry out their duty based on normal practices. Liability occurs when the normal standard of care is not achieved. It is important that contract agreements indicate the responsibility of the landscape architect to uphold a normal, and not a higher, standard of care.

Fraud is deliberate misrepresentation with the intent to deceive. Unlike negligence, it is an intentional tort. This offense can result in revocation of license to practice and possible criminal action.

Breach of Contract/Warranty

Breach of contract is a failure to fulfill an agreement made between two or more parties. A landscape architect can be exposed to liability when using a poorly written contract that does not have a clearly defined scope of services. Contract obligations must be clear and fair to both parties. The landscape architects' standard contract form should be reviewed by an attorney and professional liability carrier before being made a standard document.

Warranties can also be a breach of contract. They fall within two groups: expressed and implied. Expressed warranty is based on an explicit representation and is a part of the contract. An implied warranty is inferred by the law and is not in the contract. Landscape architects should not give warranties in their work; rather, they should indicate only that they will practice within the normal standard of care in the execution of their services. All warranties should be expressly disclaimed.

Information Provided by Others

The landscape architect may be held liable for information provided by others if the information is in error and used as a basis for work. Examples include survey data provided by the client, information provided by other consultants hired by the client, and consultants hired directly by the landscape architect.

The client has certain responsibilities on the project, including the provision of proper and accurate site data to the consultants. These data are in the form of surveys indicating the site's legal boundaries, utilities, soils, topography, and vegetation, or other information required by the consultant team. Errors or omissions in survey data may lead to incorrect design decisions. If these errors are not discovered prior to construction, they may lead to costly change orders and potential liability. The landscape architect should always conduct a visual review of the site with the client's data and highlight any potential discrepancies before proceeding with the work.

For some projects, the landscape architect is hired after the architect and engineer have already begun site planning. It is not uncommon that the architect and engineer work at different scales, resulting in discrepancies discovered only when it comes time to coordinate their information. Conflicts must be brought to the attention of the relevant parties before proceeding.

When the landscape architect hires consultants, he or she becomes responsible for their work. Consultants should be asked to provide professional liability insurance to cover their portion of the work. The landscape architect's best protection is to choose knowledgeable consultants with whom he or she has worked before.

Third-Party Liability

Third-party liability can arise when harm is inflicted on someone who is not part of the original contract between the landscape architect and the client. This can be a contractor, a subcontractor, a consultant, or an end-user of the project. Landscape architects have been prosecuted by third parties who claim personal injury or economic loss due to negligence. This may happen where codes and ordinances were not followed, plans were negligently prepared, or the site was not safely maintained during the work. A member of the general public who has an accident on the project often brings not only the owner, but also the entire project team into litigation, whether a given team member had anything to do with the alleged fault or not.

Contractors can also claim delay of schedule, which may include cost implications, because of errors and omissions on drawings or poor judgment in the issuance of site instructions. Landscape architects must practice within the guidelines of the law. Questions or legal concerns that arise should be discussed with an attorney and the state board at the earliest possible time. The best defense against liability is having a risk management and quality control plan in place, maintaining carefully prepared contracts, and thoroughly checking construction documents. An ounce of prevention is worth a pound of cure.

"The best way to reduce liability is to know your client and develop a strong relationship with them."

———————
Thomas Pritchett, Landscape Architect

Summary

This chapter discussed the definition of landscape architecture and why licensing is relevant in the profession. The requirements for becoming a landscape architect were specified, as were the ethical, legal, and liability aspects of the profession.

CHAPTER 2

Scope of Services

This chapter discusses the typical scope of landscape architecture services. It covers practice diversity past and present; forms of practice; typical project services; and collaboration with other professions.

PRACTICE DIVERSITY

The practice and diversity of landscape architecture has grown enormously since the birth of ASLA in 1899. The roots of the profession can be traced to ancient Egypt, to a tomb wall painting showing the house and grounds at the court of Amenhotep III (c. 1400 B.C.). Other early remnants of landscape architecture were found in the hanging gardens of Babylon (c. 600 B.C.) and the outdoor theaters of ancient Greece.

In the middle ages, Persian and Islamic influences were seen in the landscape of Spain. In the fifteenth and sixteenth centuries, during the Italian Renaissance, the designs of the Villa Medici, Villa d'Este, and Villa Lante all clearly manipulated the landscape in architectural form with the use of terraces and water gardens. This approach was carried into France in the sixteenth and seventeenth centuries at Vaux-le-Vicomte and Versailles. Architectural lines extending from the building, geometry, and manipulation of the land were all part of the period's landscape design. These gardens clearly influenced English formal design of the 1700s and even the planning of Washington, D.C., in 1791.

In the eighteenth century, English landscape design began a romantic movement that blended the classical lines of geometry with informal gardens. Classical elements were used in pastoral settings, and the landscape character was poetic and picturesque. 'Capability' Brown, an English gardener and designer, influenced Thomas Jefferson's design for his estate at Monticello, Virginia, and the design for Birkenhead Park in Liverpool influenced Frederick Law Olmsted's Central Park in New York City.

The term *landscape architect* was coined by Olmsted in 1858. With Olmsted's projects, including Central Park, Brooklyn's Prospect Park, the Boston parks system, and the plans for Riverside (Illinois), landscape architecture was underway as a profession in the United States. In 1899 the ASLA was formed and, in 1901, the first university program in landscape architecture was created at Harvard in Cambridge, Massachusetts.

The twentieth century saw an increasing number of trends in the profession. From the parks movement in the early 1900s, modernism in landscape design was practiced by Garrett Eckbo, Dan Kiley, and James Rose at the Harvard School of Design. Modernism was a key influence on other landscape architects, including Thomas Church and Roberto Burle Marx.

In the 1950s and 1960s, a trend in 'consumerism' was reflected in the development of theme parks. Landscape architecture was becoming an accepted profession outside of public and large private sector projects. In the late 1960s and 1970s, environmental concerns influenced planning and design, a trend led by Ian McHarg and Lawrence Halprin, among others. In the 1980s, a movement of 'art in the landscape', dominated by designers such as Peter Walker, Martha Schwartz, and George Hargreaves, influenced the direction of the profession.

It is clear that, over time, trends in landscape architecture have been developing and changing more rapidly. Influences and directions that used to take centuries to spread now do so in mere decades due to technology, new materials, and global communication.

Today, many landscape architects specialize in particular facets of the profession while maintaining landscape design and site planning as a fundamental core. Landscape architects are found in public and private practice positions as well as in academe and corporations.

The following list categorizes landscape architecture project types into five groups: landscape design, site planning, urban and regional landscape planning, specialty projects, and ecological planning.

1. Landscape Design
   - Single-family residential
   - Multi-family residential
   - Commercial
   - Industrial parks
   - Hotels and resorts
   - Memorials
   - Plazas
   - Parks design and planning
   - Greenbelts and paseos
   - Playgrounds and recreation areas
   - Streetscapes
   - Pedestrian malls
   - Rooftop landscapes
   - Rural landscape design
2. Site Planning
   - Site assessment
   - Conceptual master planning

- Feasibility studies
- Resort and community planning
- Subdivision layout and planning
- Site analysis
- Maintenance programs
- Design guidelines
- Land use planning
- Historic preservation
- Development studies
- Park system planning

3. Urban and Regional Landscape Planning
   - City and regional planning
   - Natural resource analysis
   - Environmental impact statements
   - Visual analysis
   - Landscape reclamation
   - Coastal zone management
   - Environmental management programs
   - Scenic corridor evaluation
   - Highway corridor analysis
   - Roads and highway planning
   - Zoning analysis
   - New town planning
   - Transportation studies

4. Specialty Projects
   - Regional and national park studies
   - Wildlife parks and zoos
   - Theme parks
   - Skate parks
   - Water parks
   - Golf courses
   - Elderly housing gardens
   - Public housing gardens
   - Security design
   - Therapeutic gardens
   - Sports facilities planning
   - Campus planning
   - Research and development

5. Ecological Planning
   - Site suitability analysis
   - Federal wetlands regulations
   - Brownfield development studies
   - Landfill reclamation
   - Water treatment facility planning

- Stormwater management
- Hydrological studies
- Watershed analysis
- Ecosystem health studies
- Fire ecology
- Urban-wildlife interface
- National forest management
- Wildlife refuge planning
- National resource preservation
- Landslide studies
- Land subsidence studies

Employment for landscape architects varies widely and includes roles in the private-sector; public-sector (including federal, state, and local governments), academic sector; and related industries.

In the private sector, landscape architects can work on a wide variety of projects with different client bases. Working in the private sector provides a diverse exposure to different project phases, and more important, to how a project is built. In the public sector, the landscape architect can work for federal, state, regional,

It is enlightening to step back and review the diversity of projects I have been involved with as a landscape architect. During my student years, I began doing planting designs for a landscape contractor, including the installation labor. As an apprentice later in my career, I worked alongside landscape architects, architects, and engineers and have been involved in projects ranging from small, intimate gardens to regional environmental analysis. I am still excited to work on any type and scale of project and feel that maintaining that diversity is important to keeping in touch with the many elements of the design process. The knowledge of color, form, and texture essential in a small garden design is quite different from that required in planning or urban design. It is just this type of variety that provides interest and challenge in the profession.

Not only scale but also a working knowledge of other disciplines is required. Many landscape architects and civil engineer services have overlapping duties in stormwater management, grading, and vehicular design. Civil engineers and landscape architects are both stronger when they work together to provide the best possible functional and aesthetic solutions. Landscape architects also work with architects in site planning, building orientation, and indoor/outdoor relationships of buildings and landscape. The landscape architect should also become familiar with the principles of geology, soil agronomy, horticulture, and hydrology so as to design within these parameters.

county and city agencies. The vast opportunities and types of agency are too numerous to delineate here. Duties, responsibilities, and services depend on the agency and the landscape architect's level of expertise. Public-sector tasks may include administrative duties, policy planning operations, and coordination work.

The academic sector allows the experienced landscape architect to teach on a full-time or part-time basis. A full-time tenured position normally involves not only teaching and research but also administrative, community service, and continuing education duties. Part-time teaching opportunities are found at the adjunct, lecturer, and instructor levels.

Landscape architects can be employed in related industries, including leisure and tourism; the green industry, including nurseries, irrigation, maintenance, and horticulture; the construction industry, including design/build or project management; real estate development; and architecture and engineering organizations.

The wide-ranging educational requirements of landscape architects and the broad scope of services they perform yield a generous range of employment opportunities in many industries as well as specialization within the profession.

FORMS OF PRACTICE

The organization of the landscape architectural firm depends on the number of employees, the size of its projects, and gross revenue. The company can be organized as a sole proprietorship, partnership, corporation, limited liability company, or joint venture.

A sole proprietorship is a one-owner business, with employees who can be hired to work under the proprietor. There is no limit to the size of the company. Although the advantage of sole proprietorship is lower taxes on profits, the proprietor is personally responsible for all business debts. All business expenses are deductible, and all income is taxable. The owner personally assumes full liability for any litigation against the company.

A partnership can be formed by two or more people, with each partner equally responsible for all profits or losses of the company. All partners are personally liable in the event of litigation. To form a partnership, an agreement is signed indicating the rights, terms and conditions, and responsibilities of each individual partner. An attorney should be used to draft partnership agreements that comply with governing laws.

A corporation is a separate legal entity owned by stockholders who share in profits or losses depending on their percentage of shareholdings. The corporation is created in a particular state and must abide by that state's laws. To practice in another state, a certificate of authority may be required. Corporations may be for-profit, nonprofit, or professional.

A corporation is made up of a board of directors elected by the shareholders. The board appoints officers to handle the daily operations of the company. The directors and officers may be one and the same. The individual shareholders are not personally liable for litigation against the corporation. Taxes are paid annually, and profits are distributed to the shareholders as dividends based on percentage of ownership.

Another type of corporation is the *S*-type, which allows the profit from income to be passed directly to the shareholders, who then declare it on their personal income tax returns. This avoids double taxation. The S-corporation provides the same personal liability protection as that of a regular corporation; however, business losses may affect personal assets.

A limited liability company (LLC) combines some of the tax advantages of a partnership with the personal liability protection of a corporation. LLCs avoid the double taxation of standard corporations. They do not pay taxes on profits; rather, the members pay taxes based on percentage of ownership.

A joint venture can be formed when a project or projects are too large for one firm to handle independently. An agreement is undertaken that assigns the responsibilities of each party and the amount of profit or loss to be shared. Joint ventures can be fully integrated, creating a new organization, or nonintegrated, so that the two organizations function separately.

COMPANY STRUCTURE

Every company has a hierarchy of management and control. Obviously, a sole proprietor is a jack of all trades, handling everything from directorial responsibilities to clerk and file duties. Larger companies establish a tier system with job descriptions and pay rates for each level of employment. A typical company structure is seen in Figure 2-1. Each organization assigns responsibilities, tasks, and a place in the chain of command to the employees. A company manual is critical, especially for new employees, to learn the protocol of the firm.

PROJECT SERVICES

With the variety and diversity of project types undertaken by landscape architects, the services they provide share basic commonalities. These include the preparation of detailed plans, studies, and project specifications. The project scope of services typically involves a series of phases in order to complete the plans and documents for construction purposes. These phases are:

1. Data collection phase
2. Conceptual design phase
3. Design development phase
4. Construction document phase
5. Bid/Tender phase
6. Construction observation phase

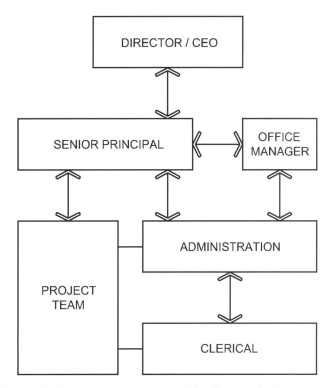

Figure 2-1   Typical company structure. This diagram indicates a structural hierarchy of management indicating lines of protocol in a typical landscape architectural firm.

Projects may include all or some of these phases depending on client requirements, project size, and scope of work. Figure 2-2 illustrates a typical project process through the office.

Data Collection Phase

Assuming all contractual issues are resolved, work on the project begins with the collection of data. This is to establish constraints, guidelines, codes, and ordinances that affect the project prior to undertaking the design. Survey data are generally provided by the client or obtained through city or governmental agencies. In some cases, the landscape architect assists the client in hiring subcontractors to produce the necessary information. The culmination of data collection includes:

- Legal data: Boundary surveys, setbacks, rights of way, zoning, deed restrictions, and covenants, including identifying governmental requirements, procedures, and submissions
- Planning data: Roads, utilities, structural elements, adjacent land use, easements, and future developments

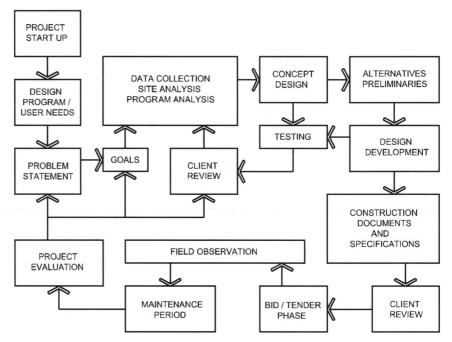

Figure 2-2 Typical project process. This diagram indicates common phases of work of a project through a landscape architectural office.

- Environmental data: Topography, soils, geology, hydrology, climate, and vegetation
- Perceptive data: Views, spatial characteristics, noise, photographic record, and positive and negative aspects of the site
- Project budget analysis and economic feasibility
- Project schedule
- Project program or design brief

All the information is documented and synthesized into a site analysis plan that, used together with the client's design program, helps in formulating the conceptual design studies. The checklist tables in Part IV provide a more comprehensive list of the data to be gathered for a typical project.

Conceptual Design Phase

The conceptual design phase commences once the data collection and site analysis are complete. The landscape architect meets with the client and other consultants to discuss conceptual ideas, budgets, schedules, and scope of work. A program/design brief is prepared, indicating the needs and goals of both client and users with respect to the project. Combining the design brief and the site analysis, the landscape architect derives a conceptual theme that is transformed into plans, sections, elevations, and renderings necessary to convey the design intent.

Once the design is approved, the landscape architect writes a letter to the client indicating completion of the concept design and the intent to proceed to the next phase of work.

Design Development Phase

The design development phase is a refinement of the conceptual design. Additional detailing of plans, sections, elevations, details, and renderings is presented for client approval.

The scope of work involves establishing grading concepts and critical elevations, pavement design, selecting hardscape materials, creating a plant palette, establishing a lighting concept, and estimating probable construction costs. A review of conformance to codes, ordinances, and deed restrictions is undertaken to ensure the feasibility of the design. It may also be necessary to meet with public agencies at this stage, particularly if the design requires variances to existing codes.

Upon completion and approval of this phase, the landscape architect informs the client in writing of the intent to proceed to the construction document phase.

Construction Document Phase

The construction document phase is the assembly of all the design information into plans, details, and specifications for the purpose of permitting, bidding, and constructing the project. The scope of work typically involves production of the following:

- Landscape grading plans
- Landscape construction and layout plans
- Landscape construction details
- Landscape planting plans and details
- Irrigation plans and details
- Landscape lighting plans and details
- Landscape construction specifications and bid documents
- Estimate of probable landscape construction costs

Once the plans and specifications are complete, an internal plan checking process commences to ensure that errors and omissions are identified and corrected. Documents are then sealed to use for bidding, regulatory approvals, permits, and construction purposes.

Bidding/Tender Phase

This phase includes helping the client establish a list of contractors qualified to bid on the project. The construction documents are compiled, printed, and advertised for bid. During the process, all contractor queries are answered. Once the bids are received, the landscape architect prepares a tender report analyzing each bid. The contract is then negotiated between the client and contractor for final award.

Field Observation Phase

The landscape architect's responsibility during the field observation phase is to represent the client and to advise on whether or not the work is proceeding according to the design intent. The activities consist of conducting periodic site visits to observe the progress of the work and evaluating materials and submissions by the contractor. It is important to note in the contract that the landscape architect is not empowered to supervise or continuously inspect the work on site, unless the agreement is otherwise. The site visits should occur at critical junctures, such as approval of the positioning of hardscape features, review of forms for concrete before pouring, and confirming the location of specimen plant material and key construction items. The landscape architect should provide a written statement to the client and contractor indicating when site observation visits are crucial.

The landscape architect also is typically responsible for visiting plant nurseries to select and tag specimen plant material, issuing recommendations to the client for contractor payment, reviewing submittals, and conducting a completion inspection and maintenance review.

After construction is complete and substantial completion is approved, the maintenance period begins. This normally lasts for one year. The landscape architect conducts monthly site visits and provides the client with written reports on any concerns or potential liability issues that may result from neglected maintenance.

COLLABORATION WITH OTHER PROFESSIONS

During the course of a project, the landscape architect has the opportunity to collaborate with other consultants hired by the client. The major project consultants usually include the architect, civil and structural engineers, and mechanical and electrical engineers. Other consultants that may be hired are planners, quantity surveyors, architectural lighting designers, and interior designers. All of these, together with the landscape architect, form the project team. Depending on the scope of work, the landscape architect may also hire independent consultants directly, such as geotechnical engineers, fountain and lake specialists, soils agronomists, and horticulturists.

A common pitfall in larger projects involving a large number of consultants is the failure to establish a defined scope of services. In some cases, the contracts for a given project provided by the landscape architect, architect, and engineer may have gaps or overlaps in scope of services. This will result in additional service agreements or consultant conflicts if these are not discovered by the client. It is important for the client to appoint a lead consultant to review and examine the scope of work of the team members in order to avoid these gaps or overlaps in service.

The landscape architect also collaborates with the general contractor and the landscape contractor. Although the landscape architect has no formal agreement with these contractors, the owner may stipulate that the landscape architect may undertake prescribed duties on the owner's behalf. Duties and responsibilities during the construction phase must be clearly defined in the initial contract. During construction, the landscape architect should not directly issue instructions to subcontractors hired under the general contractor. All correspondence should go through the general contractor.

What role does the landscape architect fill between architectural and engineering services?

I interviewed landscape architects from both the private and academic sectors in order to ascertain a trend of response to this question. Most identified an overlapping of certain services among the three professions. For example, landscape architects and architects both practice site planning, while civil engineers and landscape architects both prepare stormwater management, grading, and subdivision plans. Landscape architects should review state practice laws that define services allowable to practice under their title.

Landscape architects should understand the principles of architecture and civil engineering in relation to these overlapping services. They may not understand built structures as comprehensively as architects and engineers do, but they do understand physical design and environmental issues that bridge their respective fields.

"Landscape architecture is a unique profession in that it has the ability to bridge the creativity of architecture with the function of engineering . . . the flexible necessity of the landscape architect's expertise is paramount to project success."

Timothy May, ASLA

This book provides checklist tables to review for the collection of data, design requirements, scope of work, and project budgeting. All team members are responsible for coordinating their portion of the work with the other consultants and for notifying the client of any discrepancies related to contract coverage.

Regularly scheduled team meetings to discuss progress and technical issues are mandatory for all projects.

SUMMARY

This chapter overviewed the typical scope of services provided by the landscape architect. A brief history was illustrated in order to show the development of the diversity of projects now part of the profession. A discussion of business structure, organization, typical project services, and collaboration with other professionals showed how landscape architects perform and function in the service industry.

PART

II

RISK MANAGEMENT

CHAPTER 3

Identifying Common Risk Exposures

Landscape architecture, like any other business, has a certain amount of risk exposure in regards to the laws governing the profession. Within the service of the business, the two most influential documents the landscape architect signs are the service contract and the seal on the construction documents. The majority of disputes on a project derive from these documents.

CONTRACTS AND PROPOSALS

A contract is a legal agreement between two or more parties, binding them to a specified performance or action. A proposal on the other hand, is a description of services, terms, and conditions offered by one party to another. The proposal is provided initially for the client to review, comment on, and compare to other offers. Proposals are often modified in scope through review with the client to provide the exact services the client is seeking. Once the elements of the proposal are agreed on, a standard contract is provided by the landscape architect. The contract should make reference to the scope of services from the proposal. In some cases, the client has an urgent time schedule and wants the work to begin at once. A letter of intent allows the work to commence before the contract is signed. This approach gives both parties time to properly review the contract while the work is progressing.

The basic elements of the proposal vary considerably with the project's scope and size. Obviously, a small residential project is less extensive than the development of a commercial center. The typical components of a proposal are:

I. Cover letter or opening statement
II. Project title and description
III. Scope of work
    A. Data collection phase
    B. Conceptual/Schematic design phase

     C.   Design development phase
     D.   Construction document phase
     E.   Bid negotiation phase
     F.   Field observation phase
     G.   Maintenance period phase

IV. Assumptions (This section lists the assumed responsibilities of the owner and other consultants in the project. It may also include the project construction budget.)

V. Additional services (This section indicates related services not in the landscape architect's scope of work.)

VI. Consultants (This section lists subconsultants to be hired under the landscape architect.)

VII. Fees (This section indicates whether a fixed fee i.e.-lump sum, hourly fee, or percentage of construction cost fee will be used for billing purposes. An hourly rate schedule is included for any additional service requirements.)

VIII. Reimbursable expenses (This section indicates percentages to be charged for expenses to be paid by the client in addition to the specified fee.)

IX. Validity (This section indicates the validity of the proposal in days.)

X. Closing remarks and signature block

The contract is the most important document signed in the client–landscape architect relationship. The standard contract should be reviewed by the landscape architect's attorney and professional liability agent. Any deviations requested by the client in regards to liability clauses should be discussed with an attorney before signing.

The following list indicates the common items found in a service contract; however, it is not necessarily complete. Laws vary from state to state. Every contract, therefore, should be reviewed by an attorney.

Typical contract components include:

I. Parties—the date, client name and address, landscape architect name and address, and project name and address

II. Scope of work—the agreed proposal scope of services and a performance schedule

III. Basis of compensation—the total contract sum, payment terms, retainers, and the hourly billing rates for additional services

IV. Fee schedule—breakdown of fees per phase of work

V. General conditions (Different clauses may or may not apply depending on the advice of an attorney.)
     A.   Additional services
     B.   Reimbursable expenses
     C.   Compensation
     D.   Client responsibilities
     E.   Insurance

           1. Workman's compensation
           2. Professional liability insurance
           3. Property insurance to be purchased by the owner
      F. Standard of care
      G. Copyright and ownership of drawings
      H. Limitation of liability
      I. Indemnification
      J. Waiver of subrogation
      K. Termination or suspension
      L. Dispute resolution
      M. Americans with Disabilities Act (ADA) compliance
      N. Hazardous material
      O. Site safety
      P. Warranties and guarantees
  VI. Signature block—names and addresses of the client and landscape architect with signature and date lines for both parties

Aside from contracts, the second area of high-risk exposure for landscape architects is the construction document package. The construction documents are drawings, details, specifications, and reports that are certified (sealed), signed, and dated by the licensed landscape architect. These documents are intended for use in the bidding, regulatory approval, permitting, and construction of the project. The seal binds the landscape architect to perform under the rules, conduct, and other provisions of state licensing laws. Care must be taken to review these drawings since any errors or omissions may result in cost or schedule implications.

COMMON RISK EXPOSURES

Before a proposal is drafted, the landscape architect should identify risks inherent in the project. Even choosing the type of project to market, such as golf courses, rooftop gardens, and skate and theme parks all carry higher-than-normal risks. Specific sites may also present undue hazards or risks for development.

The following lists potential risk exposures categorized by project phase. Actual case studies are presented as examples.

Contract Issues

When marketing for work, choose projects wisely. Be conscious of high-risk projects, including theme and water parks, golf courses, skate parks, rooftop gardens, projects with existing water or drainage problems, and buildings with foundation problems. Discuss these types of projects with an attorney before signing any contracts to determine how to manage the additional risk involved.

Always use a written contract with an exact description of services to be performed. Pro bono services require the same contractual agreements and service as billable work. The scope of services must clearly indicate what is to be provided and identify additional and excluded services. The contract should include client responsibilities with respect to design program, site survey, legal descriptions, utility information, budgets, schedule, and engagement of other consultants necessary to complete the project. The landscape architect should inform the client of the services required to complete the project under the scope of work.

The landscape architect is responsible for the work of consultants hired under their venue and so should ensure that they indemnify the landscape architect for problems they may create. Consultants must present original copies of their certificates of insurance, including workman's compensation and professional liability insurance.

Key terms and conditions included in the contract are:

- Clear definition of the fee arrangement (lump sum, hourly, percentage) and method of payment (per month, per phase); interest rate for late payments; termination clause
- Indication of the type of insurance carried, such as workman's compensation insurance for employees, general liability insurance, and professional liability (errors and omissions) insurance
- Indication that the landscape architect is not responsible for maintenance issues and that the owner is responsible for the site after completion of the project
- Under the field observation description, the statement that the landscape architect does not have the authority to reject or stop nonconforming work but only the authority to recommend to the client the work to be rejected

Key elements of the general conditions of the contract should be reviewed by an attorney. These include:

- A statement of confidentiality indicating that all work on the project be kept private, except those portions compromising the landscape architect's legal responsibilities, court orders, or any government agency requirements
- A severability and survival clause in the event that any terms in the contract are unlawful so that the contract is legally retained, excluding only the unlawful clause
- A contract limitation of liability (LOL) clause amounting to the project fee, the amount of profit, or a specified amount not to be exceeded; based on insurance coverage and professional liability carrier recommendations
- Indication that the landscape architect will exercise a reasonable and normal standard of care when complying with ADA requirements. Do not provide a guarantee or warranty that the design will comply with ADA guidelines.

- A statement regarding the use of electronic data and computer-assisted design (CAD) files that indicates copyright and ownership of documents under the landscape architect and that the design is to be used solely for the project contracted and not to be copied on other projects without consent.
- A hazardous waste materials, environmental pollution, and toxic substances clause in case of discovery of these items after project commencement. Discovery of these items on site during construction can seriously delay the project time schedule.
- Indication of the preferred dispute resolution method, either mediation or arbitration.
- The landscape architect should not provide warranties, guarantees, or certifications for error-free design or documentation. Warranties are not typically covered under professional liability insurance.

When using a contract drafted by the client it is important to carefully review the scope of services, fees, exclusions, and clauses pertaining to liability protection. Client contracts are often one-sided in terms of liability. Scope of services in a client's contract should make reference to the agreed proposal and have a clear definition of what is included. Fees should have acceptable percentages based upon service milestones, with a renegotiation clause in case of project delay. Exclusions and additional services should match the landscape architect's standard contract.

Clauses in client contracts pertaining to liability are especially critical for scrutiny. These include limitation of liability, normal standard of care, insurance, copyright of documents, hazardous material, and dispute resolution. Beware of contracts with 'hold-harmless, indemnification, warranty, or guarantee clauses.

When a landscape architect takes over a project from another landscape architect, the owner must indicate in writing who has the copyright to the design before the work proceeds. Normally, landscape architects retain the copyright to their own designs unless they forfeit that right.

Design Phase Issues

Once a contract is signed, the greatest risk to the landscape architect is the cost, schedule, and quality of the product. Most projects that fail do so because of poor planning. Before work commences on a project, a work plan must be done indicating all the items per contract, the cost breakdown of the items, and the manpower and schedule required to produce them. The work plan should have built-in contingencies as buffers for both cost and schedule. By using the work plan, the landscape architect can easily identify any overruns on the project.

Most design phase risks are associated with information provided by the client, information provided by others, security issues, or safety issues. Be proactive at the start of the project by listing potential risks and how to manage them. Risks identified from past projects are a valuable tool.

The owner should always provide essential site data, including surveys, drainage, topography, and utility information. The owner should also approve the design program before the design is started, including a list of program elements required on the site. The landscape architect must notify the client in writing if a design request does not comply with codes or ordinances. Laws regarding negligence per se require landscape architects to conform to codes and regulations adopted by federal, state, and local governments.

During the design phase, consultants can use CAD bases or an overlay drawing system to coordinate drawings. All owner approvals and completion of each phase of the work should be documented in writing.

Security and safety are paramount with respect to the health and welfare of the public. Problems in these areas are generally related to weak or inadequate design. The landscape architect should be alert to the following issues, which are common sources of problems:

- Sufficient lighting must be designed to minimize hazards and detour crime.
- Sight visibility for security in higher crime areas should be maintained.
- Adequate warning signs should be posted at potentially hazardous areas.
- Plants with thorns, weak branching, poisonous properties, excessive tree litter, or destructive root systems should not be placed adjacent to pedestrian or vehicular circulation.
- Placement in visibility areas of plants with growth over 18 inches may cause sight obstructions to vehicles.
- Fencing around swimming pools should incorporate gates with self-locking and latching devices or, to follow local codes.
- Site planning should provide compatible adjacent uses. Items such as pedestrian trails near steep slopes can be hazardous.
- Trip hazards, such as tree grates not compliant with ADA standards, staking wires for trees near walkways, outdoor use of glazed tile, protruding service access covers in sidewalks, and sprinkler risers next to walkways, must be mitigated.
- Proper fall zones for play equipment must be provided and correct equipment specified for the intended age group.

CASE STUDY 3-1   Litigation and Need for Licensed Professionals

On September 20, 1981, Diane McShea was visiting the Audubon Park and Zoological Gardens in New Orleans with her young son. As the two were walking into the area known as the beer garden and concession terrace, they began to descend a set of steps immediately adjacent to a concession stand. As Ms. McShea attempted to descend the steps, she fell all the way from the top stair to the bottom, sustaining a broken heel bone in her left foot. She filed suit against the Audubon Park Zoological Beer Garden for negligence in design.

The stairs in question consisted of five steps descending from a walkway to a recessed area. At that time, there was no handrail available for use by patrons while descending or ascending the steps. In her deposition, Ms. McShea recalls being at the top of the stairs, suddenly falling, and then being at the bottom of the stairs.

Ms. McShea's only expert witness in this case was Wiley Poole, a retired professor of engineering at Louisiana State University with no experience in site work improvement for public works. Mr. Poole testified that the lack of handrails made the stairs defective according to the codes and standards he thought were applicable, namely the American National Standards Institute, the Occupational Safety and Health Administration, and the U.S.A. Standards building code.

Defendants presented three highly qualified experts, including Murvan M. Maxwell, coauthor of the current city building code, qualified as an expert in architecture and safety. He and the other two experts testified that the design of the series of steps in question fell within the norm of the basic precepts of practice in landscape architecture: (1) They have wide and comfortable treads (14 inches); (2) the steps have less than a 6-inch rise; and (3) they are constructed of concrete with a rough broom finish. This construction allows good traction all the way to the end of the steps and is slip resistant.

The court determined that the lack of a handrail on the steps in question did not create an unreasonable risk of harm and dismissed the case.

Impact

This case shows the importance of using licensed landscape architects for projects designed for high traffic flow and public use. The case was dismissed because all applicable codes and standards were met and the project was completed in accordance with standard landscape architectural practices. While accidents are not completely preventable, more serious harm could have resulted had the steps in question had not been designed to the current codes and standards. Our litigious society is ready to file suit for any slip and fall, and building owners are wise to use licensed practitioners qualified to perform such work.

Source: Southeastern Fid. Ins. Co. v. Cashio, Cochran & Assoc., 6231 (La. App. 4 Cir 3 16 87).[9]

CASE STUDY 3-2

In Hunt v. Hatch, the negligent design of stormwater drainage caused excessive amounts of water to be discharged from a shopping center parking lot into the adjacent street. A driver swerved to avoid the torrent, lost control, and was rendered quadriplegic by a spine injury after colliding with oncoming traffic. The designer paid an undisclosed amount to settle the case.

Source: Hunt v. Hatch, No. E20623, 41 ATLA L. Rptr. 63 (Ga., Fulton Cty. Super. Ct., Apr. 24, 1997) (subsequent to settlement with the designer, jury trial resulted in $26.8 million award against the shopping center owner).[10]

Construction Document Phase Issues

Prior to initiating the construction document phase, a mockup drawing set indicating the type of drawings and details should be done. This may vary from contract requirements due to size or scale of the project, plan area enlargements, or other revelations during design. During the drafting of the construction documents, milestones for plan checking should be done at 50, 75, and 100 percent completion. At 50 percent completion, verify all base information, notes and drawing standards. At 75 percent completion, the landscape architect should review the drawings with the designer to verify that all design criteria have been met. At 100 percent completion, the principal-in-charge should check the drawings using the checklist tables provided in Part IV of this book.

During plan checking, the following items should be reviewed:

- Double-check grading and drainage plans to ensure positive runoff and sufficient pipe sizing. Drainage problems are the most common reason the landscape architect is called to the site.
- Have all structural systems checked by a structural engineer and get a copy of the calculations for the project file.
- Ensure that standard office details conform to the latest ADA guidelines.
- Review consultant drawings to ensure coordination between bases.
- Review cross-referencing between plans and details.
- Be sure that information displayed in drawings and specifications is shown one time only to prevent conflicting information.
- Verify architectural floor plans to the engineer's footprint.
- Check specification sections referencing other sections to ensure cross-references are included.
- Check for the inclusion of a clause in the specifications that the contractor is responsible for site safety. Worker injuries on the job site may result in litigation against not only the contractor but the project team as well.
- During all phases, orderly project recordkeeping should be maintained and all internal and external communication documented. After all meetings, a conference report should be sent to participating parties to relay facts and clear any misconceptions.
- When including 'supplied by owner' notes on plans, make sure it is indicated who will install the product and who is responsible for warranties.
- Before issuing an estimate of probable construction costs to the client, check for the inclusion of a clause stating that the unit prices provided represent an opinion of probable construction costs only. The landscape architect has no control over the cost of materials, labor, equipment, contractor procedures, or competitive bidding of contractors. He or she should advise the client to set aside a contingency fund to cover costs of change orders, discrepancies, or omissions during construction. Budget overruns may cost the company time to redesign the project at its own expense.

Construction documents should be thorough and complete, as they affect bid pricing and scheduling. Seal only those drawings required under the rules and regulations of the governing board. Make record copies of issued drawings, especially CAD drawings, due to the possibility of information being electronically altered. Issue all drawings with a copyright indication. Ensure the proper drawing status stamp is used when transmitting to other parties.

CASE STUDY 3-3

The consequences of negligent outdoor lighting specifications have proved lethal. In the Florida case of Batz v. First Florida Development, Inc., a homeowner was killed attempting to adjust a landscape light fixture at his residence. A lawsuit resulted, naming as defendant the landscape architect responsible for producing the lighting plan. The family of the electrocuted victim claimed that the landscape architect's improper specifications and negligent inspection had caused the wrongful death. The landscape architect paid $1,000,000 to settle the negligence claim.

Source: Batz v. First Fla. Dev., Inc., No. 97-667 CA (Fla., Martin Cty. Cir. Ct., June 4, 1993).[11]

CASE STUDY 3-4

The case of Winsted Land Development v. Design Collaborative Architects, P.C., involved a landscape architect in charge of a multidisciplinary team. The client retained the landscape architect's firm to ascertain the need for permits and obtain all permits necessary to develop a large property as a commercial center. The landscape architect failed to inform the firm's client that a U.S. Army Corps of Engineers dredge and fill permit would be needed, resulting in 6.5 acres of wetlands filled in violation of the Clean Water Act. The commercial project was stalled and lost potential tenants and buyers when the wetlands violation was discovered. The court noted that the client relied on design professionals held out to be licensed and competent, and found the design firm, through the actions of its landscape architect, to have breached a professional standard of care in not properly addressing wetland requirements. The design firm was liable for breach of contract, negligence, and negligent misrepresentation and ordered to pay a total damages award of $1,516,719.

Source: Winsted Land Development v. Design Collaborative Architects, P.C., No. CV 960071571, 1999 WL 639942 (Ct., Super. Ct. of Conn., Aug. 12, 1999).[12]

CASE STUDY 3-5

A landscape architecture firm engaged in a national scope of practice failed to diligently research and specify corrective measures for soil problems. Awarding the client $900,000 in damages, the court in that case found the firm negligent in the preparation of plans and negligent in recommending to the client to accept a bid that did not include necessary work.

Source: American Manufacturers Mutual Insurance Co. v. Edward D. Stone, Jr. & Assoc., 743 F.2d 1519 (11thCir. 1984).[13]

Bid Phase Issues

Unless the owner has already selected a contractor, the landscape architect should make sure to prequalify the bidders, verifying that they have done projects of the same or greater scope. Most landscape architecture firms have a preset list of contractors to use for competitive bidding. In public bidding, different bidding requirements may render different rates for labor and materials. The landscape architect should verify that cost estimates allow the contingency for potentially higher bids.

During the bidding, conduct pre-bid as well as post-bid meetings to answer any contractor queries. Treat all bidders equally and make sure a copy of all queries and replies is sent to every bidder. Once the bids are received, if the low bid is differs by more than 10 percent from the second lowest, analyze the rates carefully. The contractor may have left something out of the bid.

Common issues to be aware of after bids are submitted:

- Late bids should not be accepted.
- Check bid forms and unit pricing for incomplete submissions.
- Check if bid forms are signed.
- Check for bid errors in computing.
- Check for contractor exceptions, stipulations, or qualifications to the bid.

Field Observation Phase Issues

The greatest risk exposure during the construction phase has to do with budget, schedule, site safety, submittals, and flaws and defects. The project budget and schedule are the most paramount issues to the client. Drawings should be reviewed with the contractor prior to construction in order to answer any queries. Errors or omissions in the drawings observed by the contractor should be immediately resolved.

The project schedule can be jeopardized by change orders, weather, unforeseen sub-surface conditions, supplier delivery delay, work of sub-contractors, or the contractors method of construction. The contractor must provide of schedule of work prior to commencement of construction. The schedule should allow for contingencies, so that overruns can be accommodated within the set completion date.

Site safety should always be the responsibility of the contractor. This should be spelled out clearly in the bid documents. This will avoid potential litigation against the client and landscape architect for the contractor's negligence.

Contractors often claim delay in the schedule due to late approval of submittals and shop drawings. Inform the contractor in writing that any submittals will require at least 7 days for review and comment.

During the construction of a project, common flaws and defects show up repeatedly, many of which go unnoticed until after construction is complete. Pointing these out to the contractor early minimizes dismay later. These common problems include:

- Water problems and negative drainage flows, including temporary drainage backups
- Clogging of drains, pipes, and weep-holes due to construction litter or soil intrusion
- Punctures in waterproofing, filter fabric, or other membranes
- Concrete slump tests and core samples not performed frequently enough, especially for structural components such as footings and retaining walls
- Wood left exposed to weather before installation and treatment
- Application of sealants to wet surfaces
- Poor finished welding or weak welds at structural joints
- Trees located over proposed underground utilities or overhead power lines
- Garbage left in planters and excavated planting beds

These problems can usually be avoided with proper site management. The contractor should be notified beforehand that such construction flaws are not acceptable. During construction, coordinate site visits with the contractor to prevent site work being covered up or completed incorrectly. Identify critical junctures of the work and schedule timely site visits by providing the contractor a list of milestones for site visits.

When certifying payment to the contractor, the landscape architect should include a clause indicating that the certification for payment is only a recommendation to the client. The payment is recommended based on site observation, and the landscape architect cannot warranty or verify that the work claimed or invoiced by the contractor has been completed, as the landscape architect does not act as an inspector or a clerk of the works.

Upon completion of the project, the landscape architect should issue a written report that, in his or her opinion, the construction work generally complies with the design concept. Avoid issuing certificates of completion that certify the work was completed in accordance with the plans and specifications. Because the landscape architect does not act as a full-time inspector, he or she has no way of knowing whether or not the work is fully compliant with the specifications. Failure to discover and report defects during substantial completion, however, could lead to liability issues later.

After construction completion, the landscape architect should make a photographic site record and copy the photos to the client. These can usually be used to determine if problems that develop are due to poor installation or maintenance practices.

Maintenance/Post-occupancy Phase Issues

During the maintenance period, the landscape architect should make monthly site reviews and notify the owner of any problems. The maintenance contractor should not be alerted in advance to such visits, as sometimes the site is neglected until just before inspection. It is a good idea to visit the site after a hard rain to check for drainage or erosion problems. The most common reasons the landscape architect is called to the site during the maintenance period are:

- Irrigation overspill on sidewalks or roadways
- Plant material that dies for an unknown reason
- Site drainage problems or standing water areas

The most concerning risk for the landscape architect after post occupancy is third party liability claims due to injury on the site. After the one-year maintenance period, visit the site annually to be sure the design intent and appearance of the project are maintained. Note any potential hazards and send the owner a written report. This serves to limit potential liability and shows the owner your concern, which may lead to future work.

CASE STUDY 3-6   Sight Barrier Results in Death

In Harris County, Texas, Amanda Kelley, 17, was traveling to church in June 1994 when the Hallum family, driving a Chevrolet Suburban and pulling a boat, broadsided Ms. Kelley's car in an intersection. She died 15 minutes later.

The jury in the case found that the Fairfield Village Community Association, Association Management, Inc. (Fairfield's management company), and the Spencer Company (the landscaper responsible for maintaining the common areas of the development) were negligent for designing, creating, and maintaining a dangerous condition in the median at the intersection of Mason Road and Highway 290. They contended that the design, consisting of a dirt berm and tall plants, created a sight barrier between motorists heading west on 290 and motorists heading south on Mason Road. Plaintiffs claimed Ms. Kelley was unable to see Mr. Hallum as she approached the intersection, thus preventing her from taking evasive action to avoid being hit by Mr. Hallum as he went through. Hallum maintained there was not enough time in the light sequence to stop and alleged the outgrown plants in the median prevented him from seeing Ms. Kelley.

Although the original plans were done by a licensed landscape architect, the design was altered by Fairfield, AMI, and the Spencer Company without the landscape architect's knowledge. The original plans specified different plantings that would not have impeded visibility. The landscape architect was absolved of any wrongdoing in the case.

Impact

This case demonstrates the clear impact on the public's health, safety, and welfare when the design of a landscape architect is not implemented or maintained to specification. In this case, this negligence resulted in the tragic death of a 17-year old girl. The utilization of the expertise of a landscape architect would have prevented the intersection from becoming a public hazard.

Source: Norman Kelley and Jan Kelley, Ind. & on behalf of the estate of Amanda Kelley, Deceased and A N F of Matthew Kelley, a minor vs. Lloyd Thomas Hallum, Fairfield Village Community Association, Association Management, Inc., The Spencer Company (Harris County District Court 80th, Case No. 94-46155).[14]

CASE STUDY 3-7   Unnecessary Anchor Wire Causes Injury

A senior citizen was attending a concert with several friends in Philadelphia. Upon exiting the concert hall in a misty rain, she became confused about the location of the tour bus she was to take. She asked directions from another bus driver, and when she turned around to move toward the proper bus, she caught her foot under a wire, tripped, and fell on her wrist and knee, breaking the wrist and bruising the knee. Reconstructive surgery was required to repair the break.

The wire anchored a newly planted tree to its cast-iron grate. The grate was nominally 3 by 6 feet, and the wire was attached to the outside corner of the grate, approximately 4½ feet from the trunk. The wire was unmarked, and with the misty rain, light conditions were not ideal. Several people testified that the wire was not readily visible.

The tree was a replacement for one that had died, and the original design landscape architect was not consulted. The landscape contractor and owner's representative discussed the need for a stabilizing wire and relative safety of such in a high-traffic pedestrian area. The contractor testified that flagging ribbon was placed on the tree when planted but that it was removed.

As expert for the plaintiff, Carl Kelemen testified that: (1) the wire was unnecessary, given that the tree was in pavement and a tree grate of some 700 pounds was resting on the root ball; and (2) if wires were truly necessary because of vandalism, high winds, etc., then alternative methods that did not create a tripping hazard were in order. Mr. Kelemen concluded that the owner was negligent for directing the contractor to use wires when such use clearly posed a safety hazard to pedestrians.

Impact

This case demonstrates the impact that a rather small detail in an overall design can have on the public's safety. The unnecessary wire resulted in harm to the senior citizen. The situation also had a financial impact with the Philadelphia concert hall owner who paid a legal claim to the plaintiff as a result of the bad decision to use the wire.

Source: Carl R. Kelemen, RLA, ASLA, served as an expert witness in this lawsuit and provided an account to ASLA. The case was settled out of court.[15]

SUMMARY

Liability claims are rising in the landscape architecture profession. The goal of this chapter was to identify common risk exposures during the various phases of work. An identification of issues affecting not only contracts but also design, documentation, and installation were highlighted. Case studies were referenced to indicate the wide variety of claims. The next two chapters discuss how to manage risk through insurance and dispute resolution.

CHAPTER 4

Insurance

To err is human . . . to not be held liable is divine.

The purpose of insurance is to protect the office and its contents, to retain professional liability for work done, to protect work contracted through consultants, and to protect the business and its employees. This chapter discusses the most common types of insurance carried by the landscape architecture firm. Types of insurance are categorized in three groups: professional liability insurance (PLI), office-related insurance, and employee-related insurance. Criteria for selecting an insurance agent and the contract provisions to minimize risk exposure are also examined.

PROFESSIONAL LIABILITY INSURANCE

Professional liability insurance (PLI) covers exposure due to negligent acts regarding errors or omissions on documents, plans, studies, and related work done by the landscape architect. It does not cover general liability or indemnification for damages caused by others. Although not mandatory by law, because of the influx of increasing insurance claims, carrying PLI has become increasingly important for the landscape architecture firm. In addition, many clients now expect their consultants to carry PLI, including most government agencies, for which it is sometimes a prerequisite to participation in proposals.

The intent of PLI is to cover the design professional against catastrophic loss. Even a frivolous lawsuit can result in undue stress and emotional hardship, not to mention financial burden and loss of productive time. Even a victory in court does not ensure recovery of attorney fees, which can run to thousands of dollars. A judgment against the design professional for negligence could result in loss of personal assets or bankruptcy.

The PLI policy is issued on a claims-made basis rather than an occurrence basis. Claims-made insurance covers claims reported during the policy period, regardless of when the event happened. The policy covers only projects where contracts are signed after the policy is in force. If the policy is discontinued or allowed to lapse, projects lose coverage permanently.

The type of coverage varies depending on the underwriter; however, common elements to the majority of policies are as follows:

1. Coverage limits and agreements: This defines what is covered, the rights and duties of the insurance company, clarifications to claims, coverage territory and contractual liability. The term of most policies is one year.
2. Exclusions: This section varies by underwriter. Some policies do not cover attorney defense costs or independent contractor liability. High-risk projects may also be excluded from coverage. Common exclusions are criminal acts, sexual harassment, disputes over fees, and acts of war or acts of God.
3. Designated insured: The carrier provides coverage only for the licensed design professional named on the policy. The landscape architect should ascertain how to add other landscape architects in the office and new employees hired while the policy is in effect.
4. Deductible: The deductible is the amount to be paid by the design professional before the insurance company assumes the remaining cost of the claim up to the coverage limit.
5. Aggregate limit: This is the greatest amount the insurance company will pay for the sum of all claims during the policy period and extended reporting period.
6. Conditions: These are the duties and process to follow in the event of a claim. Many insurance companies stipulate a period in which to advise them of a claim made or a potential claim not yet served. Some policies have a mediation credit clause that reduces the deductible by a certain percentage provided using the mediation process is first approved by the carrier. Another condition is an insured's consent clause. This states that the insurance company will not settle the claim without the consent of the insured; however, the insurance company will not pay for any amount over and above what the claim could have been settled for.
7. Definitions: This section defines the terms used within the policy.

Annual premiums vary with geographical location, number of professionals covered, gross annual income, deductible chosen, and coverage limits. Other influences are the risk of the insured, the types of projects undertaken, and the history of previous claims.

When a claim is made, the design professional must inform the insurance company immediately, which verifies whether or not it is covered under the policy. If it is, the insurance company selects an attorney for defense of the claim. If the claim is not covered, the design professional must hire his or her own attorney.

INTERVIEW 4-1

The following is an excerpt from a telephone interview on May 18, 2005, with Mr. Jim Leatzow, President of Leatzow and Associates. Mr. Leatzow has over 25 years of experience in the professional liability insurance field and is one of the largest insurers of landscape architects in the world.

Why is professional liability insurance required by landscape architects?

First, municipalities and government projects all require errors and omissions insurance as a requirement for bidding. Second, many developers are now requiring everyone on their project team to have insurance.

Where are the majority of claims coming from?

The single most important aspect of liability is the quality of the contracts that landscape architects sign. Landscape architects frequently take the position that they do not need to spend the money to have an attorney review a contract drafted by the client. They read through the client's contract, and if it looks acceptable they sign it. The danger can simply be a word such as *and* rather than *or,* which opens them to high exposure even though they have done nothing wrong.

How can landscape architects limit their risk exposure?

Landscape architects are well trained and seldom make mistakes. However, when they do make mistakes, they may get sued, but in the vast majority of cases they are sued because they signed a poor contract or no contract at all. Almost every construction project gets sued sooner or later, and in many cases the quality of the due diligence pursued by the plaintiff's attorney is nonexistent. They sue anyone who even touched the project regardless of whether they did anything wrong.

When you take on a landscape architect as a new client, do you check his or her contracts and see if a quality control plan is in place?

Yes. It is part of our underwriting process to conduct a telephone interview and ask the landscape architect to submit copies of the standard contracts currently in use. We have seen firms use parts of other contracts they have seen through the years because certain language looks good, but they don't fully realize the dangers of doing that. We help guide them so they end up with a really tight contract that is fair to both parties. We also look if they have a quality control plan in place and ask them to explain that to us.

What type of dispute resolution clause should be in the contract?

Whatever your attorney thinks is best and is reviewed and approved by your insurance company. An arbitration clause may be acceptable, but many arbitrators are not experienced in landscape architectural issues.

How do you determine the policy limit and best deductible when shopping for professional liability insurance?

The typical deductible is $5,000, so the insurance company pays for everything from that point on. You should select a deductible that will not hurt you financially.

The typical policy limits are $250,000, $500,000, or $1,000,000, although some venues go to $2,000,000. A project policy can also be added to cover a specific project.

Do you have prior acts coverage?

Today's policies cover projects from the date of signing forward. They do not go back. If you have existing coverage in force with no lapses and want to change insurance companies, we respect your retroactive date. Professional liability insurance picks up projects that have the contract signed only after the date the insurance becomes effective.

How are the rates calculated for professional liability insurance?

Our program is different from others in that most other programs charge a rate times professional fees. Leatzow and Associates figures rates times headcount of professionals in the firm (subject to various modifiers) rather than gross income.

How does the claims process work?

The first thing to do is to call your insurance agent and explain what is going on. You should call the moment there is an issue or threat that may turn into a claim. Our obligation covers the cost of hiring attorneys to defend the claim.

Does the insurance company choose the attorney, or can the landscape architect use his or her own attorney?

Because the insurance company has the most to lose financially, we appoint an attorney for you depending on the state where the claim is filed. If your attorney has experience in the type of claim dispute, we talk with him or her to determine how best to manage the claim.

Does the insurance cover subcontractors and consultants?

The law says that if you are the prime consultant, you are responsible for the product. When you hire anyone, you must ensure that you have a contract and that the consultant has insurance. You must get a fresh certificate each time you hire the consultant. Do not depend on a photocopy. There must be a provision in the contract that they carry insurance for three to five years after the project is completed.

   If a developer hires a project team, the developer is responsible for the work product even though he or she did not design it.

Do you need to carry insurance for the full statute of limitations?

Most contracts require that you carry insurance from three to five years after completion of the project. The statute of limitations is virtually nonexistent. There was a case in California where a woman who tripped and fell on a street manhole cover sued the landscape architect who did the project fifteen years earlier, even though the road had been repaired several times.

What about protection after retirement?

That is called *tail coverage.* It is designed for either retirement or disability for a sole proprietor. It typically lasts for five years after the date of actual retirement.

What happens if you miss a payment?

Professional liability is on a claims-made basis. If you drop the insurance and a claim comes in the next day, it is as if you were never insured. If you let the policy lapse, you lose your coverage.

What are the typical exclusions in the policy?

Criminal acts, fraud, subcontractors' or consultants' work, and acts of war; acts that are not in connection with your usual service or normal standard of care; claims made against an entity owned or managed by you.

Does the policy cover you for projects worldwide?

The policy covers you worldwide provided the claim or lawsuit is carried out in the United States.

What about joint venture projects?

A true joint venture is when you file a joint venture tax return. If you do, we cover your joint venture as a separate entity. Collaboration, on the other hand, is covered to the extent of your existing coverage.

Is the policy renewable if the company has a number of claims during the period?

There is no stock answer. If you have had claims, we ask questions at the time of renewal and look at what you are using as a contract. We recommend how to prevent future claims.

Due to the cost of PLI, many landscape architecture firms look into alternatives. Some choose either no insurance ("going bare"), while others seek indemnity from their clients for specific projects. Others put a limitation of liability clause in their contract; however, these do not help against third-party claims.

OFFICE-RELATED INSURANCE

Office-related insurance policies include general liability insurance, property insurance, automobile insurance, and umbrella policies.

General liability provides coverage for liability and damages that arise from the firm's general business activities. The relevant areas are contract law, commercial law, injuries occurring at the office, and theft. These policies are quite different depending on the underwriter, so it is important to review both coverage and exclusions when comparing.

Property insurance policies differ depending on whether the business owns the building, has a mortgage, or is renting. Location is also a factor. The property insurance policy should cover risks associated with damage to the building, rebuilding costs due to fire, weather damage, theft, replacement of furniture and equipment, computer damage, inventory replacement, valuable papers, and business interruption.

If the business property is owned or mortgaged, then all of these pertain. If the office is rented, it is important to review with the landlord the coverage under his or her policy and fill any gaps. For the home-based business, the same insurance agent should handle both the homeowner's policy and the business property. The typical homeowner's policy does not cover business-related activities at home, so the carrier must be notified that the home is used for business purposes. The policy should cover office equipment in the home. If the business requires a separate storage facility for archives, the insurance must be extended to cover the items stored.

Automobile insurance should be carried when vehicles are used for the business, including employees' personal cars. Coverage should extend to the individual driving, accompanying passengers, and the company. These three scenarios should be addressed:

1. Rental cars: hired auto liability coverage. If your company is incorporated and you rent cars for business use, this insurance is required. This is in addition to any collision damage waiver (CDW) purchased from the rental car agency.
2. Employee-owned vehicles: non-owned auto liability coverage. This covers employee vehicle liability when personal cars are used for business errands and travel.
3. Company car: business auto policy. This covers a company vehicle used for business purposes. In addition, the extended non-owned auto policy should be purchased to cover any passengers riding in the vehicle.

Umbrella policies can be purchased to achieve higher policy limits for coverage against third-party liability, attorney defense costs, and gaps in general liability coverage. Most umbrella policies are sold in addition to general liability coverage and should be purchased through the same agent. Premium costs of umbrella policies are low because they do not cover small claims normally covered under the general policy. Umbrella policies vary in coverage type and limit, so collaboration with the agent is necessary to ensure gaps are filled. Most policies are sold in increments of $1,000,000. If the business is planning on doing work outside the United States, it is important to notify the agent to make sure the policy covers worldwide services.

EMPLOYEE-RELATED INSURANCE

Employee-related insurance consists of workman's compensation; group hospitalization and major medical; COBRA; group life and accidental death and dismemberment; employee practices liability; employee benefit liability; unemployment; long-term care; short term disability; long-term disability; dental; and retirement options.

1. Workman's compensation: This covers employees for bodily injury and property damage due to an accident at the office or during the course of work at the job site. Workman's compensation is independent from group hospitalization or major medical coverage. It is a program of benefits provided by the state to which an employer pays premiums in order to cover medical bills and lost wages due to injury.

    Employee liability gap coverage is usually available under the workman's compensation policy. This defends the company against claims brought by a third party who suffered damages or injury due to the actions of an employee.
2. Group hospitalization and major medical: Medical coverage, costs, and policy limitations vary widely between insurance carriers. Fee-for-service plans have

costs shared by the employer and employee. They have deductibles but allow the employee to select the doctor of their choice. Managed care plans such as preferred provider organizations (PPOs) and health management organizations (HMOs) have associated provider doctors. Premiums are lower than for fee-for-service plans, but employees must choose a doctor participating in the plan in order to get the discount.

3. COBRA: COBRA insurance (mandated under the Consolidated Omnibus Budget Reconciliation Act of 1986) is provided by businesses with twenty or more employees, which must offer an extension of health coverage for up to eighteen months after termination of employment. In certain circumstances, this can be extended up to thirty-six months. The employee must pay for the coverage.

4. Group life and accidental death and dismemberment: This is normally part of the group hospitalization/major medical policy or disability insurance policy.

5. Employment practices liability: This insurance protects the company from risks of alleged employee mistreatment, including sexual harassment, job discrimination, and wrongful termination. Check the policy for coverage concerning defamation, invasion of privacy, and misrepresentation.

6. Employee benefit liability: This insurance protects the company from errors in managing the group insurance program. There are several government mandated requirements for managing employee benefits that should be discussed with the group insurance agent.

7. Unemployment: Unemployment insurance covers employees against loss of job due to termination. It is paid for annually by the employer to both the federal and state governments.

8. Long-term care: This non-mandatory insurance covers nursing home and assisted living expenses. Coverage should be lifetime and guaranteed renewable. The insurance company selected should have a long history in this type of coverage. Most company insurance plans do not cover long-term care, so individual landscape architects or company executives may consider to purchase this policy separately.

9. Short-term disability: Short-term disability covers from eight days to 26 weeks of disability. After this period, long-term disability coverage is required.

10. Long-term disability: This policy picks up where normal medical or short-term disability coverage ends. Long-term disability can cause major financial loss due to medical expenses, potential rehabilitation costs, and loss of income. Most policies cover 50 to 66.6 percent of the salary before the disability. If long-term disability is not covered by the employer, the employee may consider purchasing it separately.

11. Dental: With the rising cost of dental care, this is a good policy to consider. Many health plans now offer this inclusive with the group medical insurance for a small additional cost.

12. Retirement: When an employee retires at age 65, federal Medicare insurance provides basic medical coverage. Many retirees also purchase supplemental

policies to cover gaps in the Medicare policy. These should be reviewed with an insurance agent.

When an employee retires between the ages of $63\frac{1}{2}$ and 65, the COBRA continuation provides coverage for up to 18 months, until age 65. COBRA health coverage is complex in its requirements and options and should be discussed with an insurance agent before considering retirement policies.

SELECTING AN INSURANCE AGENT

When soliciting for insurance, the first step is to understand the coverage that is needed. Once a checklist of coverage is made, the task of selecting the proper agent can begin. Ask other landscape architecture firms and consult with the local ASLA chapter for a list of agents who represent landscape architects. Make sure the agent has experience in dealing with the service industry. Compare insurance companies and shop for coverage rather than price. Get at least three quotations and ask for a list of references.

Attempt to get one insurance agent to cover all business areas (excluding PLI) in order to avoid gaps in coverage. Sole proprietors should ask the agent to cover their personal needs as well. An alternative is to hire an independent agent as a risk manager to provide an insurance strategy, review contracts, avoid insurance loopholes, and review and update the policies annually. This incurs additional cost but is worth considering.

CONTRACT PROVISIONS

Once an insurance agent is selected and the policies are in place, the agent should review the clauses of the landscape architect's standard service contract that pertain to coverage. An attorney must also review the contract to ensure that it conforms to state laws. Clauses in the contract to which insurance coverage is relevant include:

- Workman's compensation.
- General liability
- Professional liability

Any provision in a client's contract that mentions warranties, guarantees, or indemnification must be reviewed by an insurance agent and attorney. When hiring independent consultants, verify that they have coverage for workman's compensation, professional liability, health, and disability. The independent consultant should provide the landscape architect with original certificates of insurance before beginning work.

Summary

This chapter provided an overview of insurance issues that are relevant to the landscape architect's business. Insurance is important to minimize financial loss due to unforeseen events. The landscape architect must work as a team with an insurance agent and attorney to develop a concise and fair contract and to meet insurance needs.

CHAPTER 5

Dispute Resolution

This chapter describes dispute resolution methods and their processes and addresses their advantages and disadvantages. Disputes are different in every scenario; therefore, potential claims should be reviewed with both an attorney and professional liability insurance agent.

Disputes can be resolved in the conference room, through mediation, through arbitration, or by litigation. In most cases, disputes that arise between parties of the project team can be resolved in the conference room. Some disputes require an impartial third party to assist in resolution through mediation or arbitration. A very low number of disputes in the construction industry actually go to court; however, third-party claims due to personal injury after the project is completed are more frequently litigated.

The contract should contain a clause stating the preferred method of dispute resolution. This method can always be changed by an agreement of both parties during the course of the project. For the contractor, the method of dispute resolution is written in the general requirements of the specifications, which is approved by the client prior to bidding. The parties may also choose a method based on the dollar amount of the dispute. The statute of limitations provides that a claim must be filed within a period, specified by the state, from the date of substantial completion of the project. Depending on state laws, this period can be extended if a previous claim was filed on the same project. Detailed recordkeeping is therefore essential and should be archived for at least 10 years after project completion.

RESOLVING DISPUTES IN THE CONFERENCE ROOM

Obviously, the best way to avoid disputes is not getting involved in them in the first place. At the completion of each phase of the project, discuss with the client the firms performance and service. This should include complaints, problems, and ways to improve service. Do this personally rather than through evaluation forms, and follow up with written correspondence if necessary.

Even the most careful intentions, however, sometimes result in mistakes. When this happens, it is beneficial in both cost and time for the parties to resolve their differences in the conference room rather than through a formal dispute resolution process. Even mediation can cost in the thousands of dollars for attorney fees and time spent. The economic cost and benefit must be studied when considering dispute resolution.

When a complaint does occur, identify the issues, determine how to resolve the problem, and then act swiftly. Do not allow the client to remain angry or frustrated. In some cases offering some form of compensation, such as a service discount for future work, is a good way to show your concern for the relationship to continue. After resolving the dispute follow up in writing to document the outcome. Internally, analyze what caused the problem and how to prevent it from happening in the future.

If the dispute is within the project team but the landscape architect is not involved, he or she should remain a neutral and objective observer in the event that litigation becomes necessary. In most instances, conflicts and disputes can be resolved in the conference room. When a compromise cannot be obtained, it is necessary to consult a third party for help in resolving the issues. This can be either through mediation or arbitration.

MEDIATION

Mediation, or ADR (alternative dispute resolution), is the least costly and fastest method involving a third party in dispute resolution. It is a process whereby a neutral and unbiased mediator works with the parties to resolve their conflicts.

Mediation is usually acceptable by both parties if the financial reward is smaller than the cost of hiring attorneys to pursue the matter through arbitration or litigation. Mediation is a logical alternative when both parties are willing to compromise and the relationship on the project is to continue. Because mediation is nonbinding, if one side is not willing to negotiate, the rate of failure will be high. Mediation may also fail due to lack of preparation or evidence by either party, or incompatible relationships between attorneys on opposing sides. Mediation involves professional liability insurance (PLI) issues, so the insurance carrier should be consulted prior to proceeding.

The first step in the process is to select a person to act as mediator. The mediator need not be an expert in the field of landscape architecture or construction work, but this is usually helpful. Some companies and community service entities specialize in mediation programs. The parties should review the experience of the mediator and interview candidates. Compensation for mediator fees is typically shared equally between parties.

Once the mediator is selected, a written agreement is made explaining who is involved in the proceedings, the time and venue, and the type of information to be used as evidence. The mediator guides the parties through the process and points out the strengths and weaknesses of each case in order to reach an acceptable resolution. Meetings can be held jointly or separately depending upon the mediator's recommendation. The mediator may request for expert witnesses to assist with the proceedings, but this must first be approved by both parties. Each party is allowed to have an attorney present during the proceedings. Either party may withdraw from the proceedings at any time.

The mediator's decision is not binding and relies on the parties reaching an acceptable compromise. After a settlement is agreed on, an attorney should make the appropriate legal documentation to complete the releases. The settlement agreement should be clear about the responsibilities of each party and the time constraints for compliance.

If parties reach and sign a mediation settlement agreement, the agreement is enforceable as a written contract. If an agreement cannot be reached, the case can proceed to arbitration or litigation.

Here are the advantages to using mediation as a dispute resolution tool:

- The success rate is very high in the construction industry.
- The time involved is much shorter than arbitration. Most disputes can be resolved in a matter of days or weeks rather than months or years.
- The parties have the flexibility to decide on the venue, meeting times, and agenda.
- All evidence and documents submitted are maintained confidential and do not become a matter of public record.
- Attorney costs can be kept to a minimum, as depositions need not be prepared.
- The relationship between the parties can continue.

Here are the disadvantages to mediation:

- Mediation is nonbinding and can be terminated by either party at any time.
- The mediator is involved only to facilitate the ideas and help the parties reach an agreement. He or she does not judge on guilt, innocence, rewards, or damages.
- The decision maker for both parties must be present. Mediation often fails because the person in authority is not present.
- Mediation is sometimes not suited for disputes involving a great deal of money.
- Mediation is not suitable for cases concerning criminal liability.

ARBITRATION

Arbitration is a process whereby the parties submit the dispute to an impartial third party for a final, binding, and legal resolution. Arbitration procedures are less formal than those involving litigation. To begin arbitration the parties involved must agree, usually in the service contract, that the method of arbitration be used for dispute resolution. If the contract does not have an arbitration clause, the parties must mutually agree to pursue the dispute through arbitration. The arbitrator, or arbitration panel, hears the evidence submitted and then renders a legal and binding decision that usually cannot be appealed. As in mediation, an attorney and a professional liability carrier must be informed prior to proceeding.

Arbitration in the construction industry is normally conducted through the Construction Industry Arbitration Rules of the American Arbitration Association (AAA). The duty of the AAA is to administer the arbitration but not to act as arbitrator. The AAA provides a list of qualified arbitrators to the parties for final selection. The list is generated from individuals who are familiar with the industry. The contact information for the AAA is:

American Arbitration Association
Corporate Headquarters
335 Madison Avenue, Floor 10
New York, New York 10017-5905
Tel: (212) 716-5800
Fax: (212) 716-5905
Email: websitemail@adr.org

The process involves each side choosing an arbitrator, and then these two arbitrators choose a third as a tie breaker. This three-member panel guides the parties through the arbitration process and renders a binding decision based on the evidence submitted. The prevailing party may be entitled to compensation for attorney fees in connection with the proceedings, if this is stated in writing beforehand.

For some service companies, arbitration is a preferred solution for dispute resolution because the final decision is binding and the process is less costly than litigation. The decision through arbitration is almost always not appealed unless evidence of fraud, misconduct, corruption, or partiality can be proved. New evidence brought forward may also be used for appeal.

Here are the advantages of arbitration:

- The decision of the arbitration panel is final and legally binding.
- The process is usually less costly and time-consuming than litigation.
- The result of the proceedings remains confidential.
- The degree of negligence and compensation is decided.
- The meetings can be flexibly scheduled by the parties involved.

Here are the disadvantages of arbitration:

- The decision of the arbitration panel is final and binding.
- There are no appeals as in litigation.
- The rules of evidence may not be observed.

INTERVIEW 5-1

The following is an excerpt from a telephone conversation on June 3, 2005, with Mr. Steve Sharafian. Mr. Sharafian is an attorney with a San Francisco–based law firm who specializes in representing design professionals. He has a degree in architecture from the University of California at Berkeley and a law degree from the University of Santa Clara. He also teaches professional practice to architects, landscape architects, and engineers at the University of California at Berkeley.

Mediation

Can you give a brief overview of the mediation process?

Mediation is a nonbinding resolution process whereby a mutual third-party mediator facilitates a resolution to a problem between two parties. Parties must first agree that they will try to mediate their claim. There is no hard-and-fast rule to the process, such as in litigation, and the parties can agree on the process to be followed.

First, information is presented to the mediator, and then each side is separated for individual discussions. The mediator advises each party as to the strength of the case. The mediator's goal is to find common ground to bring the parties together and agree how to resolve the dispute.

What are the advantages and disadvantages of using mediation as a dispute resolution tool?

Mediation has been widely successful in the construction industry because it focuses parties on resolving the dispute in a nonadversarial environment. It has a very high success rate. The parties have the opportunity to pick a mediator who knows the construction industry. The time involved is quick compared to other dispute resolution processes. Even if the parties are far apart in their dispute at the start, they can usually still find common ground. More important, they can keep their records confidential.

How is a mediator selected?

A mediation service provides a list of mediators to select from. Both parties review the list and mutually agree on a specific person. Mediators can be attorneys, retired judges, or participants in the construction industry.

How is mediation enforced if it is nonbinding?

Usually the parties try to settle rather than going into litigation. Mediation does not work unless both parties mutually agree and have the intent to settle.

Can parties proceed with arbitration if mediation does not resolve the dispute?

The contract usually specifies either mediation or arbitration to resolve disputes. The industry is leaning toward contracts with mediation clauses. If the contract does not have a dispute resolution clause, both parties must agree on how to proceed.

Can the landscape architect use or reference clauses from American Institute of Architects (AIA) documents in the contract?

AIA documents are not structurally suited to landscape architects. Likewise, the AIA documents use the term *architect,* so their use by landscape architects may violate state practice or title acts.

Are attorney fees recoverable for the prevailing party?

Mediators cannot award attorney fees. The parties must sign an agreement beforehand that the losing party will reimburse these fees. The common practice is that each party pays for its own attorney.

Arbitration

Can you give a brief overview of the arbitration process?

Arbitration has some similarities to mediation in regard to the process. The chosen arbitration association has its own rules, which depend on the type of dispute.

First, there is some amount of discovery between sides in order to understand the claims. After this, an arbitration hearing is scheduled where both parties have the opportunity for opening statements, rebuttals, testimony, and cross-examinations. The arbitration panel may ask queries during the process. After all testimonies are completed, the arbitrators study all the information, render a decision, and determine the damages to be paid in a specified period. Their decision is binding and can only be appealed under limited circumstances depending on state law.

What are the advantages and disadvantages of arbitration?

The advantage of arbitration is that it is a private dispute resolution process. If the arbitrators are experienced, the dispute can be handled quickly. The disadvantage is that, like litigation, arbitration could go on for a number of years depending on the complexity of the claim.

Can arbitration be used in criminal or personal injury cases?

Not in criminal cases. Many personal injury cases, however, are handled through arbitration or mediation processes. Parties have the right to settle disputes how they best see fit.

Are attorney fees recoverable for the prevailing party?

If the parties initially agreed in the contract that the prevailing party will recover attorney fees, the arbitrators can decide who the prevailing party is. The arbitrators can also decide that there is no prevailing party, in which case attorney fees are not recoverable by either side.

General

Does the professional liability insurance provider dictate the type of dispute resolution clause in the contract?

They do not dictate, but only encourage. Many recommend contract language that can be taken to an attorney for review. Some insurance companies give credit toward the deductible for disputes resolved in mediation.

How does one minimize risk exposure for errors and omissions on drawings prepared by consultants hired by the landscape architect?

Make sure your consultants have insurance, because if they make a mistake in their services, the lead consultant is responsible. Another way to minimize risk is through a contract with an indemnification clause. However, the best way to minimize risk is to hire experienced consultants you are comfortable working with. Some problems may also arise when the landscape architect is strongly encouraged to hire a consultant through the advice of their client.

Even with insurance, if a claim is awarded for an amount greater than the consultant's coverage, the landscape architect is responsible for that amount exceeding the coverage limit.

What if the financial loss is more than the losing party can pay?

If there is insurance with reasonable limits, the award is usually settled within the limit of the coverage. An award of a claim above coverage must be negotiated between the parties involved.

Because many sole-proprietor landscape architects practice without professional liability insurance, what contract clauses should they use to minimize risk exposure?

Jurisdictions vary in regard to what they allow in terms of liability. Some states allow a limitation of liability clause in the contract specifying the limit of liability to a certain dollar amount. This does not cover third-party liability, however, and most clients are not willing to indemnify the landscape architect against third-party liability.

Some landscape architects employ practice management techniques by working only with certain clients, consultants, and contractors with whom they feel comfortable.

What are the most common liability and risk exposures for landscape architects, in your experience?

Most claims result from items involving water. We see issues having to do with irrigation problems, drainage, and rooftop leaks.

Is the testimony of an expert witness in litigation a key factor in determining the result of a case?

Yes. Negligence is proved from the testimony by other professionals. In litigation or arbitration, expert witnesses are used. The experts called on by the two sides rarely agree, and their presentation and qualifications most likely make or break a case.

LITIGATION

Litigation is "the act or process of bringing or contesting a lawsuit. A judicial proceeding or contest."[16] Litigation is a costly and lengthy process, especially because project work, schedule, and service fees are suspended during the proceedings. Cases can be tried in civil, state, or federal courts depending upon the nature of the dispute.

Costs involve attorney fees, court costs, loss of business time, loss of cash flow, and related stress. The resolution of the dispute may take months, if not years, to be finalized. Even a victory does not ensure that the winning party is reimbursed for attorney fees and court costs. Moreover, the relationship with the losing party is forever lost. In some cases the defendant may end up paying more for the defense of the claim than the actual cost of damages.

Litigation is usually undertaken when the monetary value of the case is high or when one party is seeking a large financial reward. Due to the expense of court costs and attorney fees, litigation is usually not practical unless a large monetary sum is at stake.

What should you do if you get sued?

Once you receive a formal letter from a plaintiff's attorney, your own attorney must be the one to reply. Do not attempt to answer a claim personally or to contact the party making the claim. If you have professional liability insurance, contact your agent immediately. The PLI insurance company usually assigns you an attorney. If you do not have PLI insurance, you need to get your own attorney involved. Gather all relevant documents for review. Review the events leading to the case. Do not discuss the case with anyone other than your lawyer.

The process in litigation involves a pre-trial and a trial phase. In the pre-trial phase, depositions are made, evidence is gathered and exchanged between parties, motions are made, and court conferences are attended. The defendant seeks to have the claim dismissed. If it is not, counterclaims are usually made. Motions may also be made for summary judgment.

In cases where the landscape architect is the defendant due to negligence, the plaintiff must prove that the normal standard of care was not achieved. The burden of proof for economic loss or injury is on the plaintiff.

If the case goes to trial, a jury is selected, opening statements are made, and the plaintiff's evidence is presented. The defendant's attorney cross-examines, and each party calls expert witnesses. These witnesses are usually the key factor in proving negligence. After closing arguments are made, the jury renders a verdict and the judge applies the rules of the law in determining sentence. The losing party may make a motion for appeal. If the jury is deadlocked, the result is a mistrial.

Here are the advantages of litigation:

- The final decision of the court is binding; however, the losing party can appeal.
- Litigation is usually used for cases where personal injury, major damages, or high financial rewards are involved.

Here are the disadvantages of litigation:

- Litigation is costly due to attorney fees, court costs, and deposition preparation.
- It is time-consuming and there are usually long waits between court appearances. The schedule, which can conflict with business practice hours, is set by the court.
- All the information submitted as evidence is of public record. There is no confidentiality.

EXPERT WITNESSES

Each side normally hires an expert witness to provide a professional opinion on the dispute. Such witnesses are used frequently in cases involving negligence in order to prove whether or not the landscape architect worked to a normal standard of care.

Expert witnesses are required to prepare for the case ahead of time and to be unbiased in their opinion, no matter which side they are hired to represent. It is expected that different expert witnesses be called on behalf of each side to refute the testimony of the other. The burden of proof in negligence cases may be greatly influenced by an expert witness's testimony.

SUMMARY

The best way to avoid a dispute is to keep in constant contact with the client. When things start to go awry, spend even more time talking and try to resolve the problem immediately. If the problem cannot be resolved in the conference room, prepare to discuss the matter with your PLI carrier and attorney. Do not wait until you are served with a claim.

Use concise and fairly written contracts that were reviewed by both your PLI carrier and attorney. A risk management and quality control plan should be part of normal office procedures. Have the right people doing the right job in order to minimize errors and omissions. Most important, always maintain the highest standard of ethics.

PART III

QUALITY CONTROL TECHNIQUES

CHAPTER 6

A Quality Control Plan

At the heart of litigation is the absence of quality.[17]

When the word *quality* is mentioned in the service industry, three questions immediately come to mind:

1. Isn't quality and quality control something we did in the 1990s? Isn't it passé now?
2. Isn't quality part of that ISO 9000 thing that only applies to manufacturing?
3. Isn't that quality stuff just a lot of paperwork?

First, true quality will never be out of date. This was never clearer than today, when quality in documentation is demanded by clients, lawsuits for negligence are on the rise, and striving for greater profitability and efficiency is essential to remaining competitive.

The ISO 9000 is an international quality system developed by the International Organization for Standardization (ISO), based in Geneva, Switzerland. ISO 9000 was developed to combine many international standards into a universal application of quality management principles. It does not pertain to the actual product or service but rather to the process that results in the product.

ISO standards have been developed in a series, with ISO 9000 first being published in 1987. Since then, ISO 9001 provided requirements for implementation and product quality. ISO 9002 and ISO 9003 provided requirements for meeting customer needs; these have been incorporated into ISO 9001. ISO 9004 is based on guidelines for performance improvement. In the United States, the American National Standards Institute (ANSI) represents the ISO and administers and coordinates voluntary standards systems.

Although the majority of ISO 9000 certification occurs in the manufacturing sector, there are other ISO components, such as ISO 9004-2:1991, that provide guidelines for service-oriented businesses. To explore ISO further and to find out about application and certification, the contact information in the United States is:

American National Standards Institute
1819 L Street NW, Suite 600
Washington, D.C. 20036
(202) 293-8020
http://www.ansi.org

The last question, and the one heard most often, involves the perceived massive amount of paperwork required for a quality control plan. Quality is not based on the amount of documentation but rather the process of its application to achieving the final product. Overkill in documentation is not only a burden but also is detrimental to billable profit. The process of quality must be an integral part of the system, not just in a quality manual pulled off the shelf when a project milestone is reached. A quality plan must identify the minimum resources needed to function and then identify nonessential resources to be streamlined. The plan should identify how quality will be achieved, controlled, and managed.

This chapter emphasizes defining the essential elements that affect the typical landscape architectural firm. Although each firm is different, the fundamental requirements and their relationship to quality control are the same.

QUALITY PLAN PURPOSE

Quality control should be part of an office procedural system and project process. Quality in every aspect of the company organization, management, and project performance is the ultimate goal. Quality cannot be defined or ensured. It can, however, be improved through effective communication, commitment, and education. Checklists are helpful tools, but ultimately it is the experience of the individual performing the work that defines the product quality. It is therefore important that the staff members doing the work are continually trained and educated for improvement.

Quality should be reflected in marketing, contracts, design, documentation, administration, and client service. The plan, once in place, should be reviewed and updated twice a year. The purposes of implementing a quality control plan are to:

- Obtain client satisfaction in the product and service.
- Provide greater efficiency and monitoring of work, thereby reducing production time and increasing profits.
- Minimize errors and omissions on documents to avoid repeated mistakes.
- Minimize the chance of litigation.
- Potentially reduce premiums for errors and omissions insurance.
- Ensure proper recordkeeping on projects in case of litigation.

- Provide the best service possible to the client through more competitive fees, faster production schedules, and more efficient processes.
- Improve employee performance and attitude.
- Promote a continued demand for the company's service in the market.

In *Total Quality Project Management for the Design Firm,* Stasiowski and Burnstein develop a list of 13 "rules of quality":[18]

1. Quality is defined as "conformance to requirements"—all requirements, including budget and schedule.
2. Requirements must be mutually agreed on by the client and the entire project team.
3. Requirements must be defined quantitatively so nonconformance can be measured and made visible to everyone involved.
4. The traditional concept of the project team must be expanded to include all "suppliers" (people who provide input) and "customers" (people who use the products of the work).
5. Solving quality problems requires the efforts of a broad cross section of this extended project team.
6. There must be a firmwide system to seek out nonconformances that recur from project to project.
7. Nonconformances should be expected but not tolerated. In striving for zero defects, everyone must continually reduce the number of nonconformances.
8. Nonconformances that affect client satisfaction are the most serious; they should receive the highest priority.
9. Prevention is cheaper than damage control; the earlier you catch a problem, the less costly it is to fix.
10. There must be a firmwide commitment to quality from the chief executive officer (CEO) all the way down to the most junior clerical assistant.
11. Everyone in the firm must be trained so to understand the new ways of looking at quality.
12. Individuals and groups who achieve the goals of quality improvement must be appropriately recognized and rewarded.
13. Total quality project management (TQPM) cannot be viewed as a program in addition to the firm's "normal" business; it must become the way the firm does its business.

THE QUALITY PLAN

The quality plan should begin by outlining the company policy towards achieving quality; followed by a brief statement of the firm's scope of work and description of services. A list of goals to be achieved by the implementation of the quality plan should follow, indicating a time line for implementation.

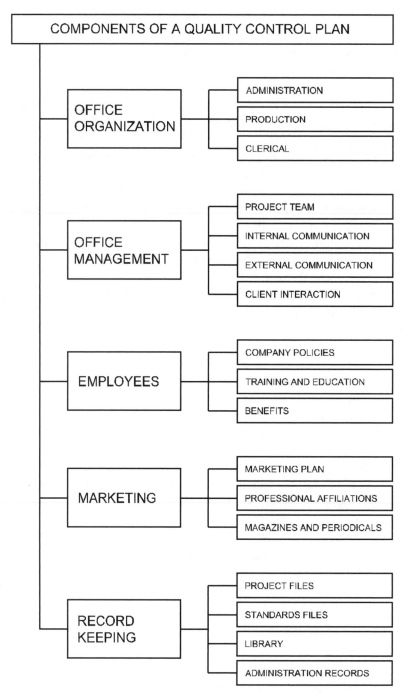

Figure 6-1   Components of a quality control plan.

The main body of the quality plan is categorized into five integral components: office organization, office management, employees, marketing, and recordkeeping (see Figure 6-1). All are equally important to office operation regardless of company size or number of employees. Management must be committed to the implementation of the quality plan and make it part of the functional process of the office. An office quality team should be established and include a member from each department having a different specialization. Management must determine the time, cost, and extent to which the plan should evolve. This plan is intended to provide a base reference outline that can be modified to meet the specific needs of the company.

OFFICE ORGANIZATION

The landscape architectural office should be organized into three distinct functional areas (or physical plant), namely administration, production, and clerical. This provides a physical and, more important, a psychological differentiation of the three functions. Figure 6-2 represents a typical office organizational diagram.

The administration area, also referred to as the front office, consists of reception, the conference room, accounting, and supply storage. This area is the first impression of the business to clients and the outside world, and is therefore imperative that it be kept and maintained in an organized and neat condition at all times. Completed project photographs and plan graphics should be displayed to give visitors an idea of the firm's work. Visitors should not be allowed into the production or clerical areas unless approved by the office manager.

The production area is the busiest and largest space in the office. Sufficient space must be allocated for staff, staff expansion, filing, and layout. Private offices for principals and a room for reproduction equipment and CAD plotters should be adjacent.

The clerical area contains the library, the plan and document file room, a marketing materials area, and material sample storage. This essential space is often underallocated in office planning and can grow quite quickly out of control. Many companies have experienced the horrors of plans stored in all parts of the office, material samples under tables, and library books and product literature buried under employees' desks.

OFFICE MANAGEMENT

Strict management is essential for the efficient flow of the project through the office. It involves appointing a project team and establishing internal and external flows of communication.

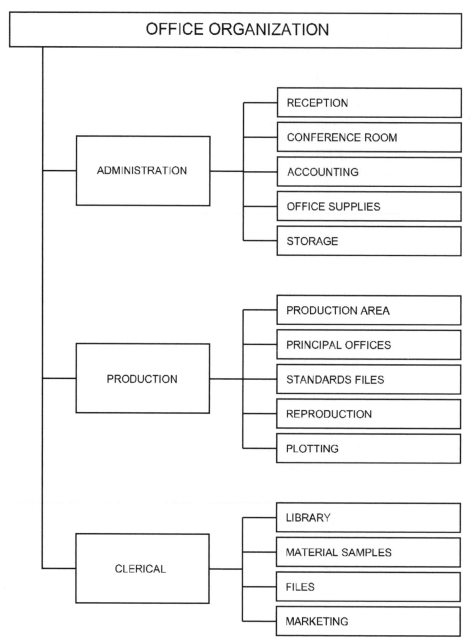

Figure 6-2   Office organizational diagram.

   The manpower required for the project team varies with the project size and schedule. Manpower planning is necessary to determine if additional employees should be hired, outside services contracted, or layoffs undertaken. In a project team approach, the team consists of the principal in charge, project manager, designer, field supervisor, three to five project staff members, and clerical support. Advantages to the project team approach is that team members stay in control of the project and are responsible for the end product; therefore, time is not lost in familiarizing other employees with the work. Figure 6-3 indicates a typical team hierarchy.

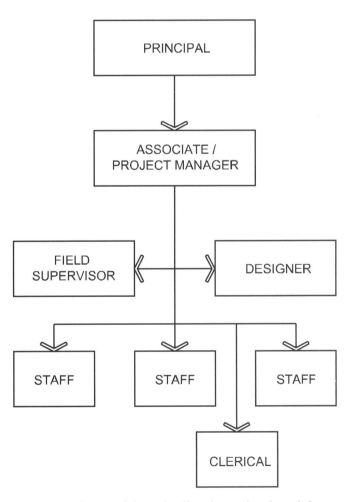

Figure 6-3   The project team. Some of the roles listed may be shared due to office structure, size, and employee experience level.

Another team structure for larger firms is the assembly line approach, which segments employees into production groups focusing their talents on a specific project phase or phases (e.g., design, production). This type of structure is almost always limited to larger firms, and although is more cost efficient, it may lead to boredom and stagnated growth for the employees.

Here are the key quality control considerations when appointing and planning the project team:

- To maximize profitability, a correct percentage of management to staff should be allocated. A project manager is usually responsible for controlling between three to five staff members.
- A work plan for the project must be established indicating manpower, scheduling, and milestones. The work plan must estimate the manpower based on billing rates. The work plan can consist of simple bar charts with milestone dates, or, for larger projects, a critical path method (CPM) may be used. The plan must allow adequate time for quality control checking and revisions prior to the project deadlines. Workload on other projects must be considered as well. Contingency time should be built in to cover holidays, vacations, sick leave, project management, and budget and schedule overruns.
- The responsibilities and expectations of each team member should be clearly defined at the project start-up meeting.
- The management and key staff should have previous experience with the project type.
- The staff should be process-oriented. They should be kept informed of scheduling deadlines and allocated hours to complete assigned tasks.
- Principal hours should be limited to key milestones during critical project stages, including contract negotiation, introduction of the project team to the client, final design presentation, construction document plan check, and certificate of completion of construction. Because principal billing rates can be three to four times that of staff, the project manager is responsible for controlling the time and billing of the principal for increased profitability.
- Each project report should be reviewed by the principal weekly. This approach quickly identifies cost overruns and scheduling problems.
- The project manager should keep records on the project team that indicate strengths and weaknesses of each employee. The records should also include recommendations for staff improvement.

Internal Communication

Internal project communication consists of team meetings related to work delegations and progress, and office staff meetings for company status and general information.

Project Team Meetings

- These meetings should be held every Monday to allocate tasks and man-hours for the week. Project process, status, and schedule are discussed. Complications or problems should be brought to the attention of the principal for prompt resolution.
- The project manager normally chairs the meeting, assigns tasks, and identifies the work expected to be completed by the end of the week. Deadlines are highlighted and overtime requirements determined.
- Clerical staff should be part of the meeting if they are to be used considerably more than normal, such as for processing specifications or reports.

Office Staff Meetings

- These should be held monthly or quarterly as determined by the management.
- The management discusses the general state of the company.
- Short- and long-term goals of the company are presented.
- Communication feedback and input from employees is critical. Memos should be circulated beforehand to ask for comments or ideas for improvement. Problems and proposed solutions should be identified and discussed.
- Information about upcoming events, seminars, and continuing education programs should be discussed.
- A company internal awards program should be established and presented.
- Outstanding service by employees and project teams should be recognized. This includes all levels of production and administrative staff.
- Completed work can be presented by the project team.
- Status reports from internal committees and the marketing department should be part of the meeting.

Office Administration Meetings

The principals, associates, and key managers should meet monthly to discuss administrative aspects of the firm. These meetings should cover:

- Marketing
- Financial report and status
- Workload projections
- Staffing requirements
- Employee performance

Quality Team Meetings

An internal quality team should be established, composed of employees with different levels of experience. A principal should head the team and be committed to implementing an officewide quality plan. The quality team should work like a project team and meet independently at regular intervals. A budget and time for these meetings and subsequent implementation should be allocated. Here are typical rules and activities for quality meetings:

- Identify current problems.
- Establish ways to solve problems.
- Assign duties and deadlines for each quality team member.
- Remain unbiased and do not place fault on individuals.
- Document results and circulate them to other principals and project managers for feedback.
- Upon officewide approval, implement quality improvements as either mandatory procedures or guidelines. These should be on a trial basis to determine the cost and benefit of the idea.
- Each project manager is responsible for overseeing the implementation of the approved quality procedure.

Introduction and implementation of a quality system takes time and may be met with criticism. Once it is effectively applied, however, the quality of drawings and cost of production will significantly improve.

Emergency Meetings

Emergency meetings may be called on specific projects due to overbudgets or delays. The project manager must review the project status weekly to ensure that it is not off course. The manager should determine why the project is over budget or late and then develop a course of action to correct the problem. This should be brought to the attention of the principal for review and approval. A staffing or scope-of-work change may be necessary to bring the project in budget. Overtime hours or hiring of subcontractors may be necessary to increase manpower to bring the project within schedule. The client must be notified if milestone dates are in jeopardy.

How to resolve budget and scheduling problems

In all the companies I have worked for, we were always pressed to meet deadlines, whether for design, construction drawings, or bidding. Most client concerns involved the project budget and schedule. Servicing clients and keeping them happy should always be top priority.

Through weekly monitoring of the project budget and schedule, problems can be quickly identified before they get out of hand. Once a problem is identified, it is best to attempt to resolve it internally before approaching the client. To overcome schedule problems, the following procedure is recommended:

1. Identify the problem.
2. Get more experienced people involved.

3. Work out a plan for overtime.
4. Determine if subconsultants are needed. It is always better to keep overtime within the project team because of the potential for increased errors and omissions due to the subconsultants unfamiliarity of the project.
5. As a last resort, ask the client what services can be extended and what are the most critical to produce first.

To overcome budget problems, the following procedure is recommended:

1. Review the scope of work and where the project is over budget.
2. Work out a plan to minimize losses.
3. Ask principals for help using their nonbillable overhead time.
4. If an item is not in the contracted scope of work, approach the client for additional services. This is always a difficult task, as most landscape architects like to provide services above and beyond that specified in the contract.

External Communication

External project communication includes collaboration with clients, consultants, jurisdictional agencies, product suppliers, and contractors. Project team members should be appointed to collaborate with outside parties. The principal and project manager should occasionally involve senior staff in external meetings as a primer for advancement and learning. Figure 6-4 represents typical external communication assignments.

Client Interaction

The expression "the customer is always right" is especially important in service-oriented companies. Client expectations should not only be met but exceeded. Clients must be contacted weekly and kept in the communication loop, especially regarding budget and scheduling issues. Project managers should occasionally query the client as to the firm's performance and the possibility of future work on other projects.

Keeping the client happy is done through tightly managing the project budget and schedule, being prepared for meetings, and promptly responding to client and consultant queries. At the end of each project phase, personally ask the client about the firm's performance. Once the project is completed, an evaluation form should be sent to the client for comments.

⊕ MAJOR ROLE

⦶ SUPPORTIVE ROLE

○ LEARNING ROLE

EMPLOYEE	EXTERNAL AGENT: CLIENT	CONSULTANTS	AGENCIES	SUPPLIERS	CONTRACTOR
PRINCIPAL	⊕	⦶			⦶
PROJECT MANAGER	⊕	⊕	⊕	⊕	⦶
DESIGNER	⦶	⦶	○	⊕	○
STAFF		⦶	○	⦶	○
FIELD SUPERVISOR	⦶	⦶	⦶	⦶	⊕

Figure 6-4 External communication assignments. Note the importance of the project manager in communication.

EMPLOYEES

A company is only as good as the people it employs. It is imperative that employees be qualified for the level and position for which they are responsible. When interviewing, make sure to follow the laws regarding appropriate questions. Asking personal, private, or unrelated questions may be wrongful or illegal. New hires should sign an employee agreement form indicating the terms of employment, responsibilities, office policy review, and grounds for termination. Appoint a staff member at the same level as a buddy to guide the new employee through the transition period. Regular training programs and outside continuing education should be encouraged for all persons in the company.

Company Policies

A company policy manual should be developed to clearly define employee positions and office procedures in order to maintain a standard of control. This is essential in the prevention of employee-related lawsuits concerning discrimination or benefits. A company policy manual should include the following:

1. Information about, philosophy, and history of the company
2. Personnel and administration: description of work hours, overtime policies, pay procedures, vacation time, holidays, sick leave, child care, personal appearance guidelines, maternity leave, equal opportunity employment, evaluation period, absences, grievances, outside employment, conflicts of interest, termination, resignation, and unemployment
3. Employee hierarchy: job classifications, descriptions, roles, responsibilities, and chain of command
4. Operations: procedures for telephone use, email, mail, safety and health, security, tools and equipment, and library use; a project and work confidentiality statement; internal and external communication procedures and quality control policies, procedures, and guidelines
5. Benefits and insurance: benefits offered by the company including health insurance, life insurance, dental plan, pensions, social security benefits, profit sharing, and annual bonuses
6. Travel on company business: procedures related to expenses, travel time, travel advances and use of vehicles
7. Professional development: company policies on payment of annual professional registration fees, participation in community services, continuing education programs, and related affiliations

Training and Education

In addition to the policy manual, a training and education program should be established for all levels of employees. The best companies have education and training goals, with an allocation of time for the improvement of office and professional skills. New technology and construction techniques require continual learning for the landscape architect. Attending educational seminars and internal training programs should be encouraged. Employees should be asked to evaluate the training programs they have attended to determine validity for future use. Training programs should include:

External education:
- Management seminars
- Computer and CAD training
- Marketing strategies
- Stress management and communication seminars
- ASLA events and local chapter meetings
- Professional affiliation seminars
- Online and continuing education sessions

Internal training and education developed by the company:
- Technical employees' comments on the workability of the design
- Regular field trips to company and competitor's projects to critique the design and detailing

- Company key personnel sharing information and giving talks on their expertise
- Talks by experts from outside sources on their specialty
- Suppliers' presentation of product information
- An awards committee that promotes projects to the ASLA national and state chapters
- A program putting employees in charge of different areas of the office, including the library, master specification and detail files, project plan files, CAD standards, design graphic standards, off-site storage files, and computer backups
- Social gatherings outside of the office
- Cultivation of a positive morale and an office environment that feels family-oriented
- Employee reviews conducted at six-month intervals to evaluate past work, short-term and long-term goals, strengths and weaknesses, and relationship to the company
- Identification and development of employee interests as specialties within the firm

Our state licensing board recently began a mandatory annual requirement for eight hours of continuing education in order to renew our license. At first I was skeptical, as I was already reading current literature to keep myself current in the profession. I proceeded to search the website for programs acceptable for continuing education credit and was amazed to find a wide variety of informative courses. After taking a few of these, I now believe strongly in continuing education programs and highly recommend them for all landscape architects. Taking them shows your employer your ambition and desire for greater knowledge; and due to frequent changes in codes, laws, and guidelines, it is important to keep up to date on issues affecting the profession.

Benefits

The more attractive the benefits a company provides, the better chance it has of enticing key personnel to join. Employee benefit policies must conform to government standards. In determining benefits, the company should consult with an experienced insurance agent to determine legal requirements and available options.

Mandatory benefits for the company and employees include health, workman's compensation, and disability and unemployment insurance. Long-term care, long-term disability, and dental insurance are optional policies. Providing retirement benefits is a way to attract more experienced personnel and encourage them to remain lifelong members of the organization. Employees render a greater contribution if they know they are there for the duration.

Benefits can be administered through either qualified or nonqualified plans. Qualified plans include either contribution plans or defined benefit plans. Contribution plans include the 401K, SEP, profit sharing, stock bonuses, and savings plans. The company maintains an account for each employee, with benefits paid on retirement or leaving the company. Defined benefit plans are set up to provide a specified amount for each employee at retirement. The amount can be fixed or based on a percentage of salary.

Nonqualified plans normally provide benefits only to owners, principals, and key personnel as determined by the directors of the company. These plans are set up to provide a deferred income during retirement.

MARKETING

A marketing plan is essential to every landscape architectural firm to develop new client relationships and maintain contact with existing clients. There is no better way to source new projects than through positive word of mouth from past clients.

The firm should allocate a specific budget for marketing, as it is generally nonbillable time. A person or team must be selected and given a specific plan, duties, responsibilities, and goals. Materials and contact strategies must be prepared beforehand. Records must be kept indicating the target market, contacts made, and when to follow up.

Typical Marketing Plan Outline

A. Mission statement and strategy:
   1. Types of services provided
   2. Areas of expertise
B. Define goals and objectives:
   1. Job description of marketing coordinator and personnel
      - Produce and update marketing materials.
      - Determine public relations strategy and community service.
      - Develop request for proposal (RFP) and proposal standards.
      - Develop mailing and contact list.
      - Submit projects for awards.
      - Define employee roles in marketing.
      - Identify market opportunities.
   2. Financial goals
      - Budget allocations for marketing
      - Goals for contract values to be generated per year
      - Timetables and milestones

C. Define target markets and geographic area:
    1. Housing developers
    2. Commercial developers
    3. Real estate companies
    4. Architects
    5. Engineers
    6. Parks and recreation departments
    7. State and federal agencies
    8. City and local agencies
D. Identify competition:
    1. Firms providing similar services
    2. Identify market niche/uniqueness
    3. Identify client needs
E. Strategy:
    1. Process for cold calls, sending mailers, interviews, and follow-ups
    2. Marketing log or calendar
    3. Budget time and costs
F. Marketing materials:
    1. Business cards
    2. Flyers and mailers—short one-page graphic description of services
    3. Brochures—distributed and discussed during initial interview
    4. CDs—laptop and projector presentations
    5. Hardcopy photos, slides, and cut sheets of recent work not in the brochure
    6. Newsletters—quarterly or semiannually
    7. Company calendar sent at Christmastime
    8. Staff resumes
    9. Project sign boards
    10. Magazine advertisements
G. Marketing tools:
    1. Word of mouth
    2. Direct mail
    3. Cold calls
    4. Newsletters
    5. Newspaper articles
    6. Holiday calendars
    7. Thank-you letters
H. Interview strategy:
    1. Organize and dry-run presentation in advance.
    2. Find out the client's interest in advance and concentrate the presentation on that project type. Show other examples of project types as well.
    3. Prepare several presentation methods, including hardcopy brochure, laptop slideshow, projector, or TV.

    4. Come out of presentation with a project to make a proposal on or another lead to contact.

    5. Send thank-you card within one week after meeting.

I. RFPs:

    1. Talk with representative prior to submission to get additional criteria.

    2. Package information to prepare:
- Answer all queries in RFP.
- Submit qualifications.
- Include resumes of key personnel.
- Provide insurance data.
- Cost proposal.

    3. Other information to shine above the rest:
- Exceptional cover graphics
- Specific site photos and analysis of problem statement
- Accompanying CD

J. Public relations programs:

    1. Publications—newspaper articles and magazines

    2. Join professional organizations:
- ASLA
- Council of Educators in Landscape Architecture (CELA)
- Community services
- Public speaking—garden clubs
- Sponsor events—golf, tennis, etc.

The marketing plan should be reviewed quarterly to determine effectiveness and necessary refinements. An identification of the elements that are not working and how to rectify them should be a continual strategy.

As a project landscape architect, I used to deal with a client's assistant manager. When we were both promoted, I was able to bring in work by having established a working relationship with that person. The lesson learned is that today's staff member will be tomorrow's manager.

Professional Affiliations

The professional organization for landscape architects is the American Society of Landscape Architects (ASLA). The mission of the ASLA is "the advancement of the art and science of landscape architecture by leading and informing the public, by serving its members, and by leading the profession in achieving quality in the natural and built environment."[19]

Another organization, directed toward education for landscape architects, is the Council of Educators in Landscape Architecture (CELA). CELA "advocates for landscape architecture programs, provides a forum for dialog about landscape architectural education, and fosters and disseminates landscape architectural scholarship."[20] A list of other organizations related to landscape architecture is at http://www.asla.org. Some of the more popular of these are:

- American Association of Botanical Gardens and Arboreta (AABGA)
- American Horticultural Society
- American Institute of Architects (AIA)
- American Planning Association (APA)
- Council of Landscape Architectural Registration Boards (CLARB)
- International Federation of Landscape Architects (IFLA)
- National Recreation and Park Association (NRPA)
- National Trust for Historic Preservation
- National Wildlife Federation
- Urban Land Institute (ULI)

Local organizations such as churches, schools, museums, botanical gardens, grass roots committees, and neighborhood associations are also good sources for marketing.

Magazines and Periodicals

The landscape architect should subscribe to literature for updates on current events relevant to the profession. These include seminars, educational activities, and the latest product catalogs. The landscape architect can also communicate expertise and ideas through articles, books, and newsletters. Here is an abbreviated list of periodicals:

- *Landscape Architecture* magazine (http://www.asla.org)
- *Landscape Architecture News Digest* (http://www.asla.org)
- *House and Garden* (http://www.houseandgarden.com)
- *Better Homes and Gardens* (http://www.bhg.com)
- *Garden Design* magazine (http://www.gardendesignmag.com)
- *Architectural Digest* (http://www.architecturaldigest.com)
- *Architectural Record* (http://www.archrecord.construction.com)
- *Architecture* (http://www.architecturemag.com)

RECORDKEEPING AND DATABASE MANAGEMENT

Recordkeeping is critical for efficiently maintaining project files, standards files, library reference materials, and administrative records. Organized and easily accessible project records, managerial data, and financial data are essential for operations and project manifests. In many cases, the success or failure of a company depends on its ability to handle paperwork efficiently.

Complete correspondence is vital for evidence should litigation occur. In many states, project drawings and records must be kept for up to ten years. In establishing a recordkeeping system, the landscape architect should list the requirements and then look for software that meets them. A system must be established that is easy to use, can be expanded, and allows for easy retrieval of information. The software system should be backed up with hardcopies.

Accounting and tax programs should match the company's accountant's or auditor's software. The accounting firm can provide a list of compatible software. The information to be included in the accounting database system is the chart of accounts, income statement, balance sheet, and cash flow analysis. Project management reports should include revenue reports, backlog reports, job costing, invoices, accounts receivable, expense reports, and time sheets.

Project Files

All projects should be filed according to a job numbering system that links to accounting, employee time sheets, and computer databases. Files can be classified by project type or alphabetically. Files required for the typical project consist of a project notebook or file, drawing files, project archives, and CAD files and backups.

1. Project notebook file: A project notebook or file should be established and segmented according to the size of the project. Small projects may require only one file, whereas large projects may include several subfiles. A project may include subfiles for:
   - Project drawing phase files: memos, transmittals, faxes, work plan, general information, telephone log, conference reports, checklists, and cost estimates
   - Project construction phase files: field observation reports, shop drawing records, material sample records, field orders, change orders, site meetings, faxes, transmittals, substitution requests, cost estimates, certificates of payment, and project evaluation forms
2. Drawing files: flat files, vertical hanging files, and rolled files. Avoid storing drawings at employee desks, as they may be hard to locate in the absence of the employee. Original drawings should be stored in a flat or vertical file that can be removed and returned daily. Many companies now use CAD and plot drawings on bond. The disk therein becomes the original drawing.
3. CAD files and backups: Back up disks of CAD work daily and store them off site weekly. This protocol ensures that any work accidentally deleted or lost is kept to a manageable minimum.
4. Project archive files: Plans no longer in active use should be rolled, labeled, and stored. Documents should be boxed and labeled. Computer and word processing disks should be filed and a backup copy sent to an off-site storage facility.

Standards Files

To minimize potential errors and maximize time and production efficiency, the office should establish a standards file for both hardcopies and computer disks. These should include:

1. Contractual forms
2. Administrative, accounting, and financial forms
3. Construction, planting, and irrigation details
4. Design and drafting graphics files for both hand and computer applications
5. Project management forms, records, and reports
6. Drafting standards, title blocks, symbols, and plan notes
7. Cost estimates and data file
8. Specifications

A master file should be kept by the office manager, in the library, and in an off-site storage facility.

Library Reference Materials

A library should be created in a separate room in the office to allow for security of reference materials and privacy during use. The library should be categorized into:

1. Books with a numbering reference and checkout procedure system
2. Periodicals and magazines
3. Product literature files stored in folders organized according to CSI MasterFormat; technical literature reviewed yearly to remove obsolete information.
4. Standards files for details, specifications, and cost estimates
5. Contact information for suppliers, contractors, and consultants
6. Building codes, city codes, ordinances, and guidelines

Administration Records

Administration records are classified into business vital records, financial records, project management reports, and personnel records. These are to be kept secure and confidential. A copy of business and financial records should also be kept with the company accountants.

1. Confidential business vital records:
   - Legal documents and corporate charter
   - Lease agreement

- Insurance records
- Business plan
2. Confidential financial records:
   - Contracts
   - Chart of accounts: balance sheet, cash flow, income statement
   - Bank statements
   - Accounts payable and receivable
   - Expenses, petty cash, supply requisitions
3. Project management reports:
   - Earned revenue
   - Backlog
   - Job costing
   - Invoices
   - Expenses
   - Time sheets
4. Personnel records:
   - Policy manual
   - Employee agreements
   - Resumes
   - Work records
   - W-2 forms and other tax information
   - Insurance
   - Termination record
   - Evaluations
5. Marketing records:
   - Marketing plan
   - Contact list
   - Proposal formats
   - Telephone logs
   - Marketing calendar
   - Marketing materials

PROCESS

Now that the components of the quality plan are identified, they must be implemented. The five steps in the process are shown in Figure 6-5.

Each of these processes will differ depending on the company's size, organization, and operations. The most vulnerable quality compromise occurs in small firms where growing pains are a negative catalyst. Insufficient manpower to meet deadlines sometimes leads to a sacrifice in quality.

In order to provide quality assurance, the quality plan must be implemented into the project process, monitored, and documented. Standardized forms, work

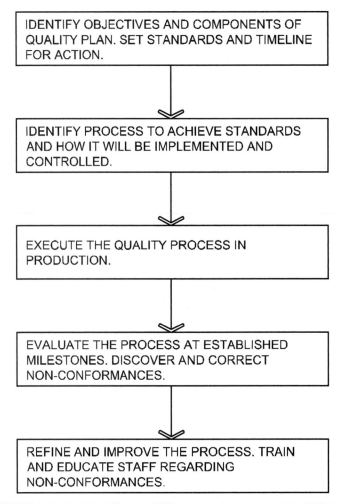

Figure 6-5   The quality control process.

plans, critical path diagrams, and checklists are essential tools for quality assurance. All staff must be educated on the processes to achieve quality and have
continual reinforcement from the management.

SUMMARY

This chapter defined the five essential components of a quality control plan: office organization, office management, employees, marketing, and recordkeeping. The details of these components should be modified based on the specific
needs of the company.

CHAPTER 7

Plan Checking Quality Control

This chapter discusses the essence of plan checking, plan review process and procedures as well as when and how to use the checklists in Part IV. The last part of the chapter relates plan checking to CAD drawings and presents issues to be aware of when using CAD as a drafting tool.

THE ESSENCE OF PLAN CHECKING

Plan checking is a procedure done at the critical milestones of a project in order to minimize errors and omissions. A good plan checking procedure can be used to improve productivity, help to educate staff, and strengthen quality control. Errors and omissions can be decreased by the use of checklist tables that allow staff to check their own work. This will reduce the amount of time spent by project managers and principals and thereby increase profitability.

It is a common misnomer to believe that plan checking is just that one percent, or less, of the contract value that is budgeted to check construction drawings prior to bidding. Plan checking should be done at every phase of the work including data collection, design, construction documentation, construction, maintenance, and project close-out. Plan checking is important today more than ever due to the increase of insurance claims and litigation in the profession. Client expectations are higher and competition is stronger. Drawings and documents must be absent from errors and omissions due to the cost implications of disputes.

Plan checking is the responsibility of the project manager and principal in charge; however, each employee should be responsible for his or her own work before submitting it to the project manager. This responsibility helps employees improve their work and saves time for the project manager in reviewing the drawings.

Utilizing both the project manager and principal for review provides an overlapping of quality control. In small firms, where the duties of the landscape architect encompass both of these responsibilities, a time interval should be allocated between the drafting and checking of the documents. At least three days should be built into the project schedule to allow for a fresh look at the drawings.

The location where plan checking is done is equally important. Obviously the office is the logical place, but the environment is more important than the location. Being away from interruptions, telephones, or pagers is vital to provide unbroken concentration. This may require going outside the office. Sufficient layout space is also a necessity for cross-checking and referencing between plans. When working with CAD, final plan checking should not be done on the computer screen. A hard copy is needed to review and mark on, as well as having a record copy of the plan check.

Why did I use to check plans in a teahouse?

I had the fortunate opportunity to work in Singapore during the Southeast Asian construction boom of the 1990s. It was a very fast-paced and progressive society on the leading edge of technology. Clients were worked hard and demanded the same of their consultants.

One of my many tasks at that time was to plan check drawings before they went out to bid. Plan checking involves correlating and cross-referencing drawings, details, and specifications. It also involves ensuring that the details are workable and relate to the design theme. Plan checking requires ample space for laying out drawings; more important, it calls for undisturbed concentration.

One day my scheduled task was to review a large drawing package. I was psychologically motivated and ready to proceed, grabbed my third cup of coffee, and spread out the drawings when the telephone rang. After that, internal office matters requiring immediate attention took about three hours, and the morning was gone.

At lunch, I walked by a teahouse located in the second floor of an old shophouse. I went up the narrow stairway in order to case the joint. At the back was a round table, plenty of floor space, and room dividers. No telephones, no potential for interruptions, and all the tea I could drink for a modest price. Bingo! I sped back to the office, grabbed the drawings, and left word that I was out for the day. By 8:00 P.M. my task was done, and the teahouse had a new regular customer.

THE PLAN CHECKING PROCESS

The appropriate checklist tables should be completed at the end of each phase of work to ensure that the documented information is complete and accurate. Part IV of this book provides checklists corresponding to typical phases of work performed by the landscape architect. Figure 7-1 indicates when each checklist table is applied and who is responsible for the documentation.

CHECKLIST APPLICATION PROCESS

PROJECT PHASE	CHECKLIST APPLICATION	WHEN TO APPLY	RESPONSIBILITY
DATA COLLECTION	1: Project Information	Project start-up	PM
	2 to 4: Data Collection/Site Analysis	On-going during phase	PM
	5: Client Questionnaire	Project start-up	Principal
CONCEPT DESIGN	6 to 15: Consultant Coordination	On-going during phase	PM / Designer
	16: Design Requirements	On-going during phase	PM / Designer
	17 to 20: Reports/Special projects	On-going during phase	PM / Designer
	21: Accessibility Requirements	Prior to design development	PM / Designer
	40: Cost Estimate	End of phase	PM
DESIGN DEVELOPMENT	6 to 15: Consultant Coordination	End of phase	PM / Designer
	16: Design Requirements	End of phase	PM / Designer
	17 to 20: Reports/Special Projects	On-going during phase	PM / Designer
	21: Accessibility Requirements	End of phase	PM / Designer
	40: Cost Estimate	End of phase	PM / Designer
CONSTRUCTION DOCS	21: Accessibility Requirements	90% and 100% completion	PM / Principal
	22 to 38: Construction Documents	90% and 100% completion	PM / Principal
	39: Specifications	100% completion	PM / Principal
	40: Cost Estimate	100% completion	PM / Principal
BID / TENDER PHASE	41: Bid/Tender	On-going during phase	PM / Principal
FIELD OBSERVATION	42: Site Observation	On-going during construction	PM / Field
	43: Maintenance	On-going during maintenance	PM / Field
PROJECT CLOSE-OUT	44: Project Close-out	End of maintenance period	PM / Principal
	45: Client Evaluation Form	End of construction	PM / Principal
	46: Project Evaluation	End of maintenance period	PM / Principal

Figure 7-1 Application of checklists during the project process. This chart indicates when to use the checklists in Part IV of this book.

Although every phase of the work is important, the most critical plan check is at the 100 percent completion of construction documents, as these drawings are used for bidding purposes and will affect costs and construction scheduling. Errors and omissions at this stage are the most frequent reason landscape architects are charged for negligence, or requiring the firm to pay for its own errors.

Larger firms generally have an office guru, usually at the principal level, who is responsible for plan checking the construction documents. Although each reviewer has a personal style and process, the checking procedure has a typical sequential process. Sequencing is important since errors in the bases, grading, or construction plans will have a rippling effect through the entire construction package. A typical procedure chart for checking construction documents is shown in Figure 7-2.

The initial step is to check the base plan against other consultants' drawings. In the past, this involved an overlay procedure on a light table, but CAD has made this task much less troublesome.

Once the base plan is verified, the grading plan is checked. The grading plan precedes the construction plan because changes in grading may affect construction layout, step risers, pad and terrace elevations, wall heights and design, and associated details. Grading details should be cross-checked with the plan. Frequently, pipes shown on details are not shown on the plans, and vice versa.

After the grading plan, the construction plan is checked and cross-referenced concurrently with the construction details. This determines if details are sufficient to build the project. A separate review of ADA requirements should be done at this stage. Any plans provided by consultants hired under the landscape architect should be reviewed against the construction and grading plans.

The next plan to check is the planting plan and details. This must be cross-checked against any revisions made to the construction and grading plans. The irrigation plan and lighting plan, with associated details, should follow the planting plan check.

After all plans are reviewed, the specifications and bid documents should have sections referenced to all plan items. Specification sections referenced to other sections must be verified for inclusion. Frequently, sections referenced in one section do not show up in the final specification.

Use of Checklist Tables

The checklist tables provided in Part IV indicate the information required during the course of a typical landscape architectural project. The checklists are intended for several purposes:

- A guide for information to be obtained
- A guide to ensure that the work has been completed properly
- A guide to minimize errors and omissions on documents
- A coordination and reference for related work

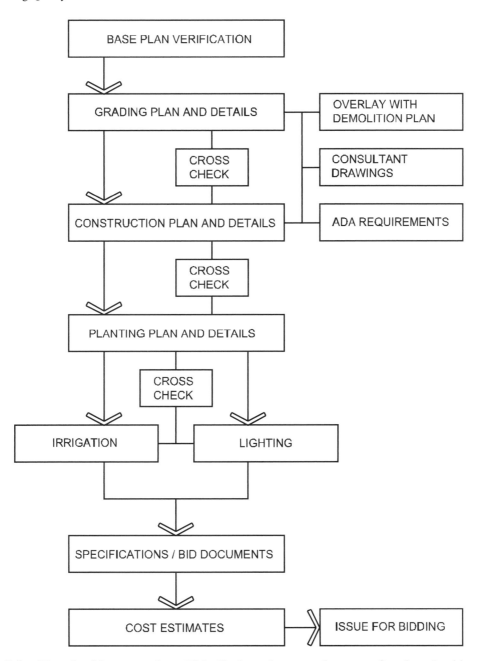

Figure 7-2 Plan checking procedure. This displays the normal process for plan checking a set of construction drawings.

The checklists provide YES and NO columns for indicating the status of the information. The NA (no answer) column should be checked if the information does not apply. Once completed, the checklist should be signed by the person in charge and kept in the project files for reference.

Each checklist was selected for its usefulness in improving quality and helpful in the project process. The checklists are not intended to provide a normal standard of care in the profession—only a reference guide to elements typical with the practice. Laws, codes, ordinances, and guidelines occasionally change or differ from state to state, and it is the duty of landscape architects to keep abreast of changes that affect their work.

Stamping Documents

Stamping indicates the status of the completed drawing set. Drawings are stamped when they are transmitted to other parties or when they are used internally as working sets. The stamps normally used during the course of the project include:

- CONFIDENTIAL: Information is not to be shared with any party other than the recipient.
- FOR INFORMATION ONLY: Used for drawings, documents, or specifications for information purposes prior to completion of the work.
- CHECK SET: Used internally for plan checking and revisions.
- FOR BID PURPOSES ONLY: Used by contractors for bidding purposes and as a basis for future cost evaluation or revisions.
- NOT FOR CONSTRUCTION: This stamp is used on completed construction documents for comments from client and consultants prior to bidding.
- FOR CONSTRUCTION: To be used once the contractor is awarded and project construction is ready to commence. Any revisions to the drawings from the bid set must be clouded and referenced in the drawing revision block.

Certifying Documents

Certifying or sealing documents is when the landscape architect's authorized seal is affixed to the drawings as required by the state regulatory board. The board normally requires the seal affixed for drawings and documents to be used for regulatory approval, permitting, or construction purposes. The landscape architect is responsible for reviewing and following the rules and regulations of the board and using the seal only when required.

Documents should be certified for work only when prepared under the landscape architect's direct supervision and control. When the work was completed by a landscape architect from out of state, it must first be reviewed for compliance with local laws prior to certification. Any modifications to be made to the plans or documents must be brought to the attention of the owner and other landscape architect prior to proceeding with revisions. Certifying drawings and documents is one of the most important legal acts performed by the landscape architect, and a great deal of scrutiny should be taken before applying the seal.

THE CAD REVOLUTION

Computer-aided drafting (CAD) has been a revolutionary drafting tool in the architectural and engineering-related service industries. The synergy of CAD and Microsoft Windows has made such programs widely recognized and user friendly. The most popular program used is AutoCAD; however, there are other programs to choose from as well.

When CAD first emerged in the 1980s, almost all landscape architects realized that this technology was the wave of the future. The benefits of CAD are the precision in drawing, repetition of symbols, and ease of communication.

It is important to find the right person to use CAD. While some people have an aptitude with the computer, others prefer design, manual drawing, working with people, or being in the field. Many experienced landscape architects who did not have the opportunity to learn CAD in school are now taking continuing education classes to keep up with today's technology.

Most companies have developed CAD procedures and standards. Company manuals state the way drawings will be set up in terms of layers, blocks, xrefs, symbols, legends, text, and dimension styles. The real benefit of CAD is the efficiency in both editing and the repetition of symbols. Standards for the architectural industry can be found at http://www.nationalcadstandard.org.

I had the opportunity to interview some CAD users and asked them about the potential exposures for errors when using CAD as a drafting tool. It is good to be aware of these issues when setting up, managing, drafting, and training employees. The project manager and principal should also be aware of these issues and review them with CAD draftspersons prior to starting the project.

General Issues

- Unless you use CAD often, the speed and proficiency of your drafting will be reduced.
- Many landscape architects find a physical distinction between designing by hand and drafting by CAD. Some can design both ways, but very few.
- Sketching design by hand allows the opportunity to go back and look at previous iterations. Some people find it hard to see the big picture when zooming in and out on the computer screen.

Sharing Information with Others

- When using bases from architects and engineers, sometimes the layers must be modified. Only partial information may be available on one layer that needs to be turned off, requiring that new layer properties be assigned.
- Consultants' plans frequently are at different scales. Correlating them may lead to conflicts.
- Consultants' plans may have graphic symbols that must be rescaled or redrawnsuch as shown in Figure 7-3.
- Do not attempt to site the architect's floor plan on the engineer's base unless this is part of the scope of services. Request that the architect coordinate with the engineer. Figure 7-4 shows a base layout per an engineer's drawing. Figure 7-5 shows the same plan with the architect's floor plan superimposed. There is more detailed information on the floor plan, which affects the layout of the paving design.
- In working with CAD, it is always better to freeze and thaw layers rather than delete them, as this information may be required in the future. Always keep an unaltered disk copy of all consultants' drawings received.

Drafting Issues

- Setting up a CAD standard manual is essential; however, if it sits on the shelf gathering dust, it will do no good. It is advisable to get feedback from the CAD users about ways to improve and streamline the standards.
- Coordination issues may become a problem when too many people are working on the same drawing. When possible, assign separate drawings to individuals rather than teams.
- Due to the clarity of CAD drawings, there is a tendency to print things smaller and add more information per sheet. Although this may save sheet quantity, it makes plan checking and adding revisions difficult. See Figure 7-6.
- Precision in drawing lines (Figure 7-7) and closing blocks properly may have an impact on measuring area sizes. An incorrectly drawn line (Figure 7-8) can result in only a portion of an area being calculated. Always verify larger areas by hand on a hardcopy print.
- In the AutoCAD program, when setting up for plotting, verify that the box 'Scale to Fit' is unchecked if the intention is to plot the sheet to a specific scale.
- Regular saves of a drawing should be done while working. Establish an office standard for time between saves.

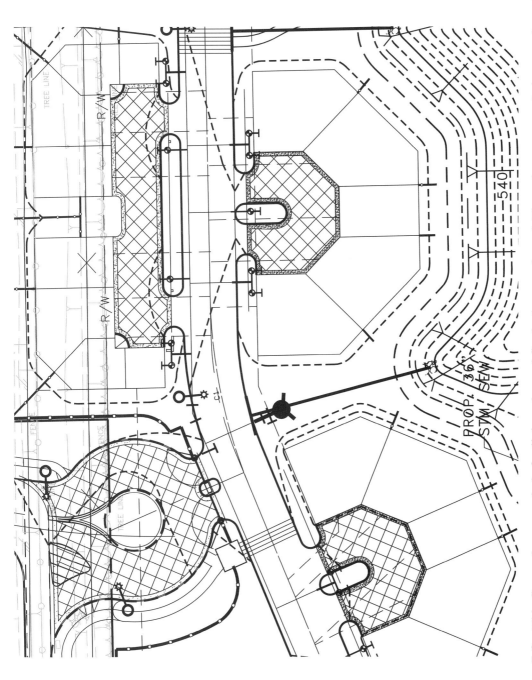

Figure 7-3 This figure shows symbols for light poles and fire hydrants enlarged. The enlargement technique works well for the engineer's drawings, but the outsize symbols are too prominent in the landscape plan. (*Courtesy of T.H. Pritchett/Associates*)

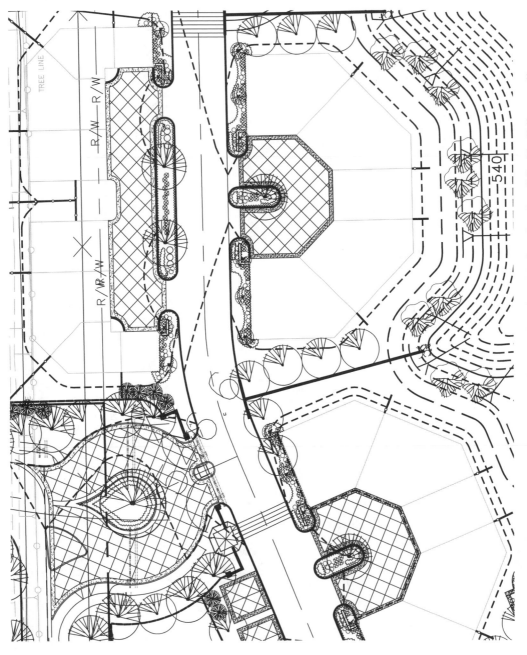

Figure 7-4 Figure shows a base layout from an engineer's drawing. Notice the simplified building outline. (*Courtesy of T.H. Pritchett/Associates*)

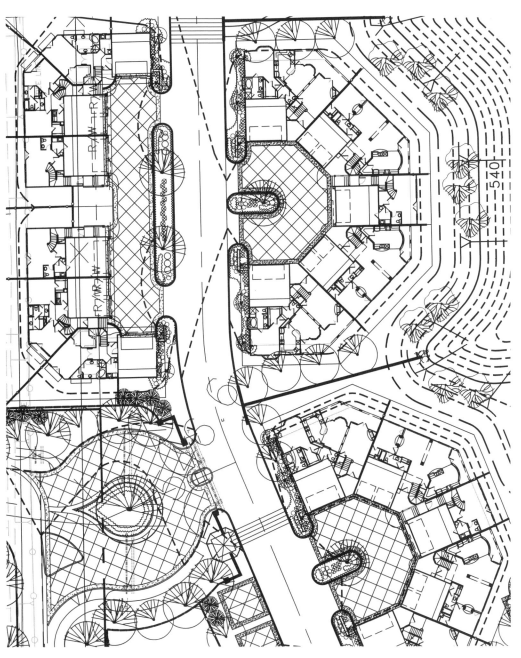

Figure 7-5 Figure shows the same plan with the architect's floor plan superimposed. The detailed information on the floor plan affects the layout of the paving and patio design if the engineer's base is used for design. (*Courtesy of T.H. Pritchett/Associates*)

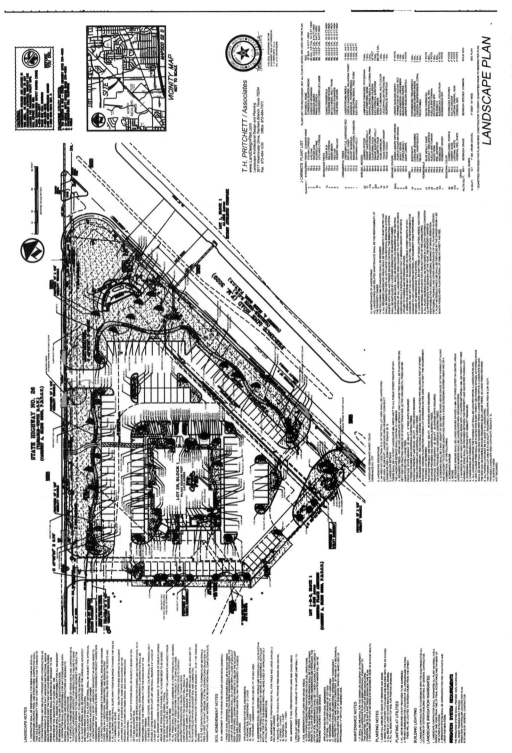

Figure 7-6 When setting up sheets, ensure that the information is legible and formatted for the intended size of the plot. Turning off some layers before plotting may improve the clarity of the drawing. (*Courtesy of T.H. Pritchett/Associates*)

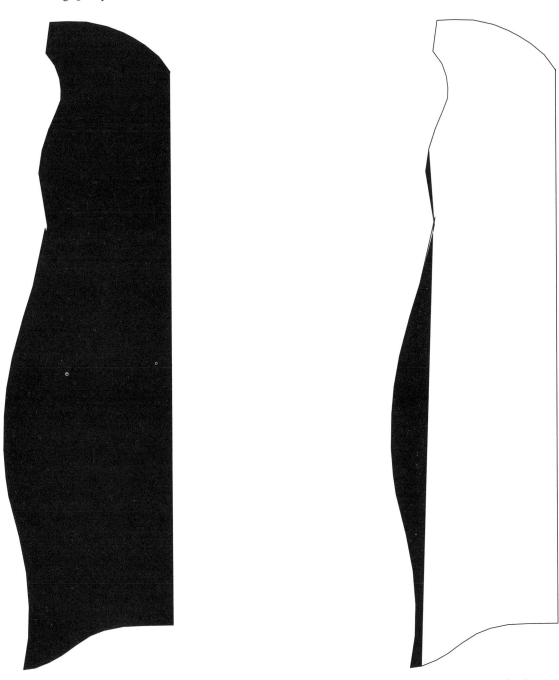

Figure 7-7/Figure 7-8 Precision in CAD drafting is essential when computing area calculations. Figure 7-7 represents a closed area that can be accurately measured and hatched. Figure 7-8 shows how one small drafting error can cause only a portion of the total area to be calculated or hatched. (*Courtesy of T.H. Pritchett/Associates*)

SUMMARY

By establishing a plan check process and procedure, documents can be reviewed more quickly and concisely. Use this process together with the checklists in Part IV to minimize errors and omissions on documents.

NOTES

1. American Society of Landscape Architects, "What Is Landscape Architecture?" (2001), http://www.asla.org/nonmembers/publicrelations/What_is_ASLA.cfm.
2. American Society of Landscape Architects, *The Practice of Landscape Architecture: Cases Impacting the Public's Health, Safety, and Welfare* (May 2002), http://www.asla.org/members/govtaffairs/licensure/pdf/phsw-final.pdf.
3. Alex P. Schatz, *Regulation of Landscape Architecture and the Protection of Public Health, Safety and Welfare.* Produced for American Society of Landscape Architects, Washington, D.C. (October 2003). (From: Mary Butler, "Fire Precautions Save Homes," (Boulder, Colo.) *Daily Camera,* November 4, 2003, 1A, 5A).
4. Schatz, *Regulation of Landscape Architecture.* (From: Ross v. Southern Cal. Edison Co., No. 257053 (Ca., Riverside City. Super. Ct. April 22, 1997)).
5. ASLA, *Practice of Landscape Architecture.*
6. Data per American Society of Landscape Architects.
7. American Society of Landscape Architects, "ASLA Code of Professional Ethics," *Leaders Handbook* (2001). http://www.asla.org/goverance/ldrshdbk/code.htm.
8. ASLA, *Practice of Landscape Architecture.*
9. Ibid.
10. Schatz, *Regulation of Landscape Architecture.*
11. Ibid.
12. Ibid.
13. Ibid.
14. ASLA, *Practice of Landscape Architecture.*
15. Ibid.
16. *The Collins English Dictionary* (HarperCollins), 2000.
17. Frank Stasiowski and David Burnstein, *Total Quality Project Management for the Design Firm* (New York: John Wiley and Sons), 1994.
18. Ibid., 43.
19. ASLA, 1993.
20. Council of Educators in Landscape Architecture, 2006. From: http://www.thecela.org

PART IV

QUALITY CHECKLISTS

CHECKLIST MASTER

Project: _____

Date: _____ Project # _____

DATA COLLECTION CHECKLISTS

Y	N	NA	
☐	☐	☐	1. CHECKLIST 1: Project Information
☐	☐	☐	2. CHECKLIST 2: Data Collection
☐	☐	☐	3. CHECKLIST 3: Site Inventory
☐	☐	☐	4. CHECKLIST 4: Site Analysis
☐	☐	☐	5. CHECKLIST 5: Client Questionnaire

CONSULTANT COORDINATION CHECKLISTS

Y	N	NA	
☐	☐	☐	1. CHECKLIST 6: Architect Coordination
☐	☐	☐	2. CHECKLIST 7: Civil Engineer Coordination
☐	☐	☐	3. CHECKLIST 8: Structural Engineer Coordination
☐	☐	☐	4. CHECKLIST 9: Mechanical and Electrical Engineer Coordination
☐	☐	☐	5. CHECKLIST 10: Quantity Surveyor Coordination
☐	☐	☐	6. CHECKLIST 11: Interior Designer Coordination
☐	☐	☐	7. CHECKLIST 12: Architectural Lighting Designer Coordination
☐	☐	☐	8. CHECKLIST 13: Fountain/Lake/Pool Consultant Coordination
☐	☐	☐	9. CHECKLIST 14: Geotechnical/Soil Agronomist Coordination
☐	☐	☐	10. CHECKLIST 15: Horticulturist Coordination

DESIGN DOCUMENT CHECKLISTS

Y	N	NA	
☐	☐	☐	1. CHECKLIST 16: Design Requirements
☐	☐	☐	2. CHECKLIST 17: Typical Report Outline
☐	☐	☐	3. CHECKLIST 18: Landscape Assessment Components
☐	☐	☐	4. CHECKLIST 19: Stormwater Management
☐	☐	☐	5. CHECKLIST 20: Urban Design Components
☐	☐	☐	6. CHECKLIST 21: Accessibility Requirements

CONSTRUCTION DOCUMENT CHECKLISTS

Y   **N**   **NA**

☐ ☐ ☐   1. CHECKLIST 22: Base Sheet

☐ ☐ ☐   2. CHECKLIST 23: Demolition Plan

☐ ☐ ☐   3. CHECKLIST 24: Construction Plan

☐ ☐ ☐   4. CHECKLIST 25: Construction Details

☐ ☐ ☐   5. CHECKLIST 26: Grading Plan

☐ ☐ ☐   6. CHECKLIST 27: Planting Plan

☐ ☐ ☐   7. CHECKLIST 28: Interior Planting Plan

☐ ☐ ☐   8. CHECKLIST 29: Lighting Plan

☐ ☐ ☐   9. CHECKLIST 30: Irrigation Plan

☐ ☐ ☐   10. CHECKLIST 31: Specialty Items: Tennis Courts

☐ ☐ ☐   11. CHECKLIST 32: Specialty Items: Swimming Pools

☐ ☐ ☐   12. CHECKLIST 33: Specialty Items: Water Features

☐ ☐ ☐   13. CHECKLIST 34: Specialty Items: Children's Playgrounds

☐ ☐ ☐   14. CHECKLIST 35: Specialty Items: Rooftop Gardens

☐ ☐ ☐   15. CHECKLIST 36: Specialty Items: Wood Decks and Trellises

☐ ☐ ☐   16. CHECKLIST 37: Specialty Items: Retaining Walls

☐ ☐ ☐   17. CHECKLIST 38: Specialty Items: Streets and Parking

SPECIFICATION CHECKLIST

Y   **N**   **NA**

☐ ☐ ☐   1. CHECKLIST 39: Specifications

COST ESTIMATION CHECKLIST

Y   **N**   **NA**

☐ ☐ ☐   1. CHECKLIST 40: Cost Estimates

BIDDING/TENDER CHECKLIST

Y   **N**   **NA**

☐ ☐ ☐   1. CHECKLIST 41: Bidding/Tender

SITE OBSERVATION CHECKLISTS

Y	N	NA	
☐	☐	☐	1. CHECKLIST 42: Site Observation
☐	☐	☐	2. CHECKLIST 43: Maintenance

PROJECT CLOSEOUT CHECKLISTS

Y	N	NA	
☐	☐	☐	1. CHECKLIST 44: Project Closeout
☐	☐	☐	2. CHECKLIST 45: Client Evaluation Form
☐	☐	☐	3. CHECKLIST 46: Project Evaluation

Recorded by: _____ Date: _____

Approved by: _____ Date: _____

CHECKLIST 1   PROJECT INFORMATION

PROJECT: _____

Date: _____ Job # _____

Site Address: _____

_____

_____

INTERNAL PROJECT TEAM

Principal: _____

Project Manager: _____

Designer: _____

Staff: _____

Clerical: _____

CLIENT

Company: _____

Mailing Address: _____

_____

Phone/Fax: _____

Email: _____

Representative: _____

ARCHITECT

Company/Contact: _____

Address: _____

_____

_____

Phone/Fax: _____

Email: _____

CIVIL ENGINEER

Company/Contact: _____

Address: _____

_____

_____

Phone/Fax: _____

Email: _____

STRUCTURAL ENGINEER

Company/Contact: _____

Address: _____

_____

_____

Phone/Fax: _____

Email: _____

MECHANICAL/ELECTRICAL ENGINEER

Company/Contact: _____

Address: _____

_____

_____

Phone/Fax: _____

Email: _____

QUANTITY SURVEYOR

Company/Contact: _____

Address: _____

_____

_____

Phone/Fax: _____

Email: _____

INTERIOR DESIGNER

Company/Contact: _____

Address: _____

_____

_____

Phone/Fax: _____

Email: _____

ARCHITECTURAL LIGHTING CONSULTANT

Company/Contact: _____

Address: _____

_____

_____

Phone/Fax: _____

Email: _____

FOUNTAIN/LAKE SPECIALIST

Company/Contact: _____

Address: _____

_____

_____

Phone/Fax: _____

Email: _____

SOILS AGRONOMIST/ENGINEER

Company/Contact: _____

Address: _____

_____

_____

Phone/Fax: _____

Email: _____

HORTICULTURIST

Company/Contact: _____

Address: _____

_____

_____

Phone/Fax: _____

Email: _____

BUILDING DEPARTMENT

Company/Contact: _____

Address: _____

_____

_____

Phone/Fax: _____

Email: _____

PLANNING DEPARTMENT

Company/Contact: _____

Address: _____

_____

_____

Phone/Fax: _____

Email: _____

OTHER

Company/Contact: _____

Address: _____

_____

_____

Phone/Fax: _____

Email: _____

OTHER

Company/Contact: _____

Address: _____

_____

_____

Phone/Fax: _____

Email: _____

Recorded by: _____   Date: _____

Approved by: _____   Date: _____

CHECKLIST 2   DATA COLLECTION

Project: _____

Date: _____ Project # _____

PROPOSED FEATURES

Y	N	NA	
☐	☐	☐	1. Information obtained from client including: program/design brief/project goals/budget/schedule/surveys
☐	☐	☐	2. Architectural plans and concept
☐	☐	☐	3. Civil engineering plans/roads/utilities
☐	☐	☐	4. Structural plans
☐	☐	☐	5. Mechanical/electrical plans
☐	☐	☐	6. Site remediation work

FEDERAL AGENCIES/REGULATIONS

Y	N	NA	
☐	☐	☐	1. National Environmental Policy Act (NEPA)
☐	☐	☐	2. Environmental Protection Agency (EPA)
☐	☐	☐	3. Clean Water Act
☐	☐	☐	4. National Flood Insurance Act
☐	☐	☐	5. National Historic Preservation Act (NHPA)
☐	☐	☐	6. U.S. Geological Service (USGS)—geology maps/geologic formations/topography/earthquake, landslide, groundwater data/flood risks
☐	☐	☐	7. U.S. Department of Agriculture (USDA)—Soil Conservation Service (SCS)-soil surveys/hydrology/plant hardiness zones
☐	☐	☐	8. U.S. Forest Service—vegetation
☐	☐	☐	9. National Weather Service
☐	☐	☐	10. U.S. Weather Bureau
☐	☐	☐	11. U.S. Army Corp of Engineers—flood limits
☐	☐	☐	12. Federal Aviation Administration—airport information
☐	☐	☐	13. Federal Emergency Management Agency (FEMA)—flood maps
☐	☐	☐	14. Americans with Disabilities Act (ADA)

☐ ☐ ☐   15. Department of Interior—wetlands maps

☐ ☐ ☐   16. U.S. Census Bureau—population/education/ethnic background information

☐ ☐ ☐   17. National Register—historic districts

☐ ☐ ☐   18. U.S. Fish and Wildlife Service—National Wetlands Inventory (NWI)/Endangered Species Act (ESA)

☐ ☐ ☐   19. Occupational Safety and Health Act (OSHA)

☐ ☐ ☐   20. Department of Housing and Urban Development (HUD)

STATE AGENCIES/REGULATIONS

Y   N   NA

☐ ☐ ☐   1. State Environmental Policy Act (SEPA)

☐ ☐ ☐   2. Department of Health—toxic disposal sites/landfills

☐ ☐ ☐   3. Department of Public Safety—road grading/drainage

☐ ☐ ☐   4. Agriculture Department—soil information

LOCAL AND CITY AGENCIES/REGULATIONS

Y   N   NA

☐ ☐ ☐   1. Building Department—building, electrical, and plumbing codes

☐ ☐ ☐   2. Planning and Zoning Departments—land use/topography/zoning/community facilities

☐ ☐ ☐   3. Health Department

☐ ☐ ☐   4. Parks and Recreation Department

☐ ☐ ☐   5. Municipal Utility Districts (MUD)

☐ ☐ ☐   6. Telephone Company/CATV

☐ ☐ ☐   7. Gas Company

☐ ☐ ☐   8. Electric Company

☐ ☐ ☐   9. Water Department

☐ ☐ ☐   10. Fire Department

☐ ☐ ☐   11. Tax Assessor Collector—tax maps

☐ ☐ ☐   12. Department of Public Works—street/drainage/topography

PRIVATE REGULATIONS

Y	N	NA	
☐	☐	☐	1. Deed restrictions
☐	☐	☐	2. Subdivision regulations
☐	☐	☐	3. Land titles

CONSULTATION WITH AGENCIES

Y	N	NA	
☐	☐	☐	1. Permitting and approval processes defined
☐	☐	☐	2. Submission requirements—plans, documents
☐	☐	☐	3. Timeline for approvals
☐	☐	☐	4. Special code requirements applicable to city obtained
☐	☐	☐	5. Subdivision regulations
☐	☐	☐	6. PUD regulations

BUILDING CODE APPLICATION

Y	N	NA	
☐	☐	☐	1. BOCA National Building Code (NE USA)
☐	☐	☐	2. Standard Building Code (SE USA)
☐	☐	☐	3. Uniform Building Code (W USA)
☐	☐	☐	4. Other _____

SUBMISSION REQUIREMENTS

Y	N	NA	
☐	☐	☐	1. Sheet size/format
☐	☐	☐	2. Sealing/signing of documents
☐	☐	☐	3. Forms to be included
☐	☐	☐	4. Fees to be included

PERMITS REQUIRED

Y	N	NA	
☐	☐	☐	1. Building
☐	☐	☐	2. Fencing
☐	☐	☐	3. Water connection/irrigation

☐ ☐ ☐   4. Sewer connection

☐ ☐ ☐   5. Storm drain connection

☐ ☐ ☐   6. Telephone connection

☐ ☐ ☐   7. Natural gas connection

☐ ☐ ☐   8. Grading/excavation/fill

☐ ☐ ☐   9. Parks and Recreation

☐ ☐ ☐   10. Curb cuts

☐ ☐ ☐   11. Retaining walls (usually over 48 inches high)

☐ ☐ ☐   12. Signage

☐ ☐ ☐   13. Temporary buildings/structures

☐ ☐ ☐   14. Awnings/canopies/tents (usually over 200 square feet)

☐ ☐ ☐   15. Street tree planting

☐ ☐ ☐   16. Tree mitigation

☐ ☐ ☐   17. Demolition

☐ ☐ ☐   18. Swimming pools

☐ ☐ ☐   19. Other _____

STANDARDS

Y   N   NA

☐ ☐ ☐   1. American Society for Testing and Materials (ASTM)

☐ ☐ ☐   2. American National Standards Institute (ANSI)

☐ ☐ ☐   3. U.S. Department of Commerce (USDC)

☐ ☐ ☐   4. USA Standards (USAS)

Recorded by: _____   Date: _____

Approved by: _____   Date: _____

CHECKLIST 3   SITE INVENTORY

Project: _____

Date: _____ Project # _____

LEGAL DATA

Y	N	NA	
☐	☐	☐	1. Land ownership/ lot/block/tract number
☐	☐	☐	2. Boundary/property line survey
☐	☐	☐	3. Deed restrictions/restrictive covenants
☐	☐	☐	4. Existing land use and zoning
☐	☐	☐	5. Rights of way
☐	☐	☐	6. Site acreage
☐	☐	☐	7. Easements/setbacks
☐	☐	☐	8. Subdivision ordinances
☐	☐	☐	9. Fire access requirements
☐	☐	☐	10. Building and safety codes (landscape structures)
☐	☐	☐	11. Plumbing codes (irrigation)
☐	☐	☐	12. Electrical codes (irrigation/lighting)
☐	☐	☐	13. Environmental Impact Statements/EPA
☐	☐	☐	14. Code requirements for permeable site area
☐	☐	☐	15. GPS survey
☐	☐	☐	16. Landscape ordinances

PLANNING DATA

Y	N	NA	
☐	☐	☐	1. Architectural buildings, structures, and elements
☐	☐	☐	2. Roads, parking areas, and driveways
☐	☐	☐	3. Pedestrian paving areas
☐	☐	☐	4. Utilities/easements/points of connection
☐	☐	☐	a. domestic and reclaimed water/water wells
☐	☐	☐	b. natural gas
☐	☐	☐	c. storm and sanitary sewers

☐ ☐ ☐   d. buried and overhead electric lines/utility poles

☐ ☐ ☐   e. cable TV

☐ ☐ ☐   f. telephone

☐ ☐ ☐   g. irrigation/hose bibs

☐ ☐ ☐   h. manholes

☐ ☐ ☐   j. traffic signals

☐ ☐ ☐   k. vaults

☐ ☐ ☐   l. light poles/transformers

☐ ☐ ☐   m. septic tanks

☐ ☐ ☐   n. hydrants

☐ ☐ ☐   5. Meters

☐ ☐ ☐   6. Signage requirements

☐ ☐ ☐   7. Service access—mail, delivery, trash collection

☐ ☐ ☐   8. Population/demographics

☐ ☐ ☐   9. Setbacks

☐ ☐ ☐   10. Permitted uses

☐ ☐ ☐   11. Fencing

☐ ☐ ☐   12. Aerial surveys

ENVIRONMENTAL DATA

Y   **N**   **NA**

☐ ☐ ☐   1. Topography/slopes/stability/erosion

☐ ☐ ☐   2. Soils/geology—tests and characteristics

☐ ☐ ☐   a. agronomy

☐ ☐ ☐   b. depth to bedrock

☐ ☐ ☐   c. subsurface/soil morphology

☐ ☐ ☐   d. core drilling

☐ ☐ ☐   e. soil strength

☐ ☐ ☐   f. landfill

☐ ☐ ☐   g. expansion/contraction

☐ ☐ ☐   h. percolation

☐ ☐ ☐   j. hardpan

☐ ☐ ☐   k. seismic considerations/fault zones

☐ ☐ ☐   l. corrosiveness

☐ ☐ ☐   m. sinkholes

☐ ☐ ☐   n. workability/limitations

☐ ☐ ☐   3. Hydrology

☐ ☐ ☐   a. watersheds

☐ ☐ ☐   b. inlets/outlets/culverts

☐ ☐ ☐   c. pipes

☐ ☐ ☐   d. swales

☐ ☐ ☐   e. erosion/sedimentation

☐ ☐ ☐   f. siltation

☐ ☐ ☐   g. floodplain

☐ ☐ ☐   h. watercourses

☐ ☐ ☐   j. water table

☐ ☐ ☐   k. water bodies

☐ ☐ ☐   l. wetlands

☐ ☐ ☐   m. detention ponds

☐ ☐ ☐   n. aquifers/water table

☐ ☐ ☐   o. groundwater recharge

☐ ☐ ☐   p. water quality

☐ ☐ ☐   q. drainage patterns

☐ ☐ ☐   r. wells/springs

☐ ☐ ☐   s. drainage from adjacent sites

☐ ☐ ☐   4. Climate

☐ ☐ ☐   a. air quality/temperature/humidity

☐ ☐ ☐   b. sun/shade

☐ ☐ ☐   c. wind

☐ ☐ ☐   d. precipitation rates

☐ ☐ ☐   e. frost line

☐ ☐ ☐   f. snow rates/rapid snow melting

☐ ☐ ☐   g. freeze/thaw

☐ ☐ ☐   h. hurricanes/tornados

☐ ☐ ☐   j. fungus/mold

☐ ☐ ☐   k. insect problems

☐ ☐ ☐   5. Existing vegetation

☐ ☐ ☐   a. trees—type, size, location, condition

☐ ☐ ☐   b. understory—type, size, location, condition

☐ ☐ ☐   c. invasive species

☐ ☐ ☐   d. hazardous conditions

☐ ☐ ☐   6. Environmental concerns

☐ ☐ ☐   a. past site use

☐ ☐ ☐   b. filling/dumping

☐ ☐ ☐   c. contamination

Recorded by: _____   Date: _____

Approved by: _____   Date: _____

CHECKLIST 4   SITE ANALYSIS

Project: _____

Date: _____ Project # _____

SITE ANALYSIS DATA

Y	N	NA	
☐	☐	☐	1. Site reconnaissance conducted
☐	☐	☐	2. Cultural factors/history
☐	☐	☐	3. Social factors—health and safety
☐	☐	☐	4. Psychological—behavior of users
☐	☐	☐	5. Physiological—biological needs
☐	☐	☐	6. Physical—design for users
☐	☐	☐	7. Circulation
☐	☐	☐	a. pedestrian
☐	☐	☐	b. vehicular, fire access
☐	☐	☐	c. bicycle
☐	☐	☐	d. service—maintenance, trash collection, mail
☐	☐	☐	8. Views/scenic quality
☐	☐	☐	9. Noise
☐	☐	☐	10. Positive/negative aspects of the site
☐	☐	☐	11. Wildlife impact—birds, fish, land mammals, rare or endangered species
☐	☐	☐	12. Community facilities
☐	☐	☐	13. Site photography record
☐	☐	☐	14. Security
☐	☐	☐	15. Aerial photography
☐	☐	☐	16. Cost implications of development
☐	☐	☐	17. Landscape character

Recorded by: _____ Date: _____

Approved by: _____ Date: _____

CHECKLIST 5   CLIENT QUESTIONNAIRE

Project: _____

Date: _____ Project # _____

GENERAL

Y   N   NA

☐   ☐   ☐   1. What are the goals for the project? Design, schedule, budget?

Describe _____

_____

_____

DRAINAGE AND GRADING

Y   N   NA

☐   ☐   ☐   1. Are there any drainage problems or standing water?

Describe _____

☐   ☐   ☐   2. Is there any water seepage into the building?

Describe _____

☐   ☐   ☐   3. Are the roof gutters draining properly?

Describe _____

☐   ☐   ☐   4. Do you have a septic tank?

Describe _____

☐   ☐   ☐   5. Are there any underground pipes?

Describe _____

☐   ☐   ☐   6. Recommend use of berms or landforms?

Describe _____

IRRIGATION

Y   N   NA

☐   ☐   ☐   1. Is there an existing irrigation system?

Describe _____

☐   ☐   ☐   2. Is an irrigation system required?

Describe _____

☐   ☐   ☐   3. Are the locations and number of hose bibs sufficient?

Describe _____

☐   ☐   ☐   4. Are there areas of ponding/standing water after irrigating?

Describe _____

PAVEMENT

Is there a need for any of the following paved areas?

Y   N   NA

☐   ☐   ☐   1. Driveway?

Describe _____

☐   ☐   ☐   2. Walkways?

Describe _____

☐   ☐   ☐   3. Patios?

Describe _____

☐   ☐   ☐   4. Curbs?

Describe _____

☐   ☐   ☐   5. Synthetic turf?

Describe _____

☐   ☐   ☐   6. Playground surfacing?

Describe _____

☐   ☐   ☐   7. Porous paving or turf block?

Describe _____

What type of paving materials do you like?

☐ Concrete   ☐ Cut stone

☐ Stamped colored concrete   ☐ Flagstone

☐ Exposed aggregate   ☐ Cobblestone

☐ Brick/interlocking pavers   ☐ Asphalt

SITE IMPROVEMENTS/AMENITIES

Is there a need for any of the following amenities?

☐ Fountains/ponds/streams   ☐ Spa/hot tub

☐ Fences   ☐ Pool

☐ Trellis/lattice   ☐ Playground

☐ Railings   ☐ Exercise stations

☐ Gates   ☐ Rock work

☐ Retaining walls   ☐ Wood deck

☐ Planters—built up   ☐ Mailbox

☐ Bridges   ☐ Pots

☐ Tables/benches   ☐ Gazebo

☐ Greenhouse   ☐ Work shed

☐ Flagpoles   ☐ Signage

☐ Sculpture   ☐ Dog/pet run

☐ Compost area   ☐ Raised beds

☐ Railroad ties   ☐ Golf green

☐ Vegetable/herb garden

PLANTING

1. When do you spend most of your time in the garden? Preferred bloom season?

☐ spring   ☐ summer   ☐ fall   ☐ winter

2. What is your favorite color of foliage/flowers?

☐ Red, orange, yellow range

☐ White, pink, magenta range

☐ Lavender, purple, blue range

☐ Any

3. Do you like fragrant flowers even though they attract bees? _____

4. Do you like edible plants and/or fruit trees? _____

5. Should poisonous plants be excluded from the design? _____

6. Do you have a preferred lawn type?

☐ Bermuda   ☐ Buffalo

☐ St. Augustine   ☐ Centipede

☐ Zoysia   ☐ Carpet

7. Type of lawn installation preferred?

☐ Seed

☐ Hydromulch

☐ Sod

8. Are there any areas to screen or hide using plant material? _____

9. Procedure for existing trees?

☐ Retain all in natural state.

☐ Selective removal.

Describe _____

☐ Pruning required.

Describe _____

☐ Clear all.

10. What type of planting design style do you like?

☐ Formal

☐ Informal/natural

☐ Mix

☐ Any

11. Are there any favorite plants you would like to use?

_____

_____

_____

_____

_____

LANDSCAPE LIGHTING

Do you require any of the following landscape lighting?

☐ Security lighting

☐ Pathway lighting

☐ Landscape accent lighting

☐ Focal/spot lighting

MAINTENANCE/OTHER

1. How often do you spend in the garden for maintenance? _____

2. Do you need an area for a children's playground? _____

3. Do you have pets? _____

Do they stay outdoors? _____

4. Do you require a one-year maintenance period after final acceptance? _____

BUDGET

1. Do you have a budget figure? _____

2. Would you like an estimated budget based on this survey? _____

SCHEDULE

1. What is the schedule for completion? Key dates?

Data collection _____

Concept design _____

Design development _____

Construction documents _____

Bid/Tender _____

Commence construction _____

Complete construction _____

SURVEY REQUIRED

☐ 1. Boundary/Utility

☐ 2. Topographic

☐ 3. Geotechnical

☐ 4. Soils Agronomy

☐ 5. Tree/Vegetation

☐ 6. Other _____

OTHER COMMENTS

_____

_____

_____

_____

Client signature:_____   Date: _____

Recorded by: _____   Date: _____

Approved by: _____   Date: _____

CHECKLIST 6   ARCHITECT COORDINATION

Project: _____

Date: _____ Project # _____

SITE INFORMATION

Y	N	NA	
☐	☐	☐	1. Surveys
☐	☐	☐	2. Zoning
☐	☐	☐	3. Deed restrictions
☐	☐	☐	4. Easements
☐	☐	☐	5. Setbacks
☐	☐	☐	6. Permits required
☐	☐	☐	7. Building services—utilities including electric, gas, water, sewer, cable TV, telephone

DESIGN INFORMATION

Y	N	NA	
☐	☐	☐	1. Parking requirements, including disabled parking
☐	☐	☐	2. Accessible routes for disabled
☐	☐	☐	3. Emergency access—fire, ambulance
☐	☐	☐	4. Covered drop-offs and walkways to building entries
☐	☐	☐	5. Threshold and footing details
☐	☐	☐	6. Finish floor levels
☐	☐	☐	7. Building footprint
☐	☐	☐	8. Door and window locations and height of windowsills
☐	☐	☐	9. Color coordination
☐	☐	☐	10. Building style
☐	☐	☐	11. Roof overhangs and gutters/outlet points/drainage
☐	☐	☐	12. Interior and exterior planter boxes/waterproofing
☐	☐	☐	13. Basement waterproofing and drainage
☐	☐	☐	14. Garden rooftops
☐	☐	☐	15. HVAC locations

☐ ☐ ☐   16. Building signage

☐ ☐ ☐   17. Building exterior lighting

☐ ☐ ☐   18. External power supply points

☐ ☐ ☐   19. Hose bibs on building walls

☐ ☐ ☐   20. Parking garage structure, circulation, and ventilation requirements

Recorded by: _____ Date: _____

Approved by: _____ Date: _____

CHECKLIST 7   CIVIL ENGINEER COORDINATION

Project: _____

Date: _____ Project # _____

UTILITIES

Y	N	NA	
☐	☐	☐	1. Storm drain locations, manholes, pipes, connections, catch basins, inverts, easements
☐	☐	☐	2. Sewer locations, septic tanks, pipes, connections, inverts, easements
☐	☐	☐	3. Potable and nonpotable water lines and easements
☐	☐	☐	4. Natural gas lines and easements
☐	☐	☐	5. Meters—electric and water; size and locations
☐	☐	☐	6. Transformers
☐	☐	☐	7. Traffic signals and street signage
☐	☐	☐	8. Overhead lines and poles
☐	☐	☐	9. Hydrants
☐	☐	☐	10. Overlay proposed tree locations for conflicts

DRAINAGE

Y	N	NA	
☐	☐	☐	1. Site perimeter levels
☐	☐	☐	2. Subsurface geology/structural soils
☐	☐	☐	3. Floodplain
☐	☐	☐	4. Watershed analysis
☐	☐	☐	5. Water table/aquifers
☐	☐	☐	6. Soil stabilization/erosion control/siltation
☐	☐	☐	7. Compaction levels (90 percent max. in planting areas)
☐	☐	☐	8. Stormwater management plan

ROADS

Y	N	NA	
☐	☐	☐	1. Classifications and speed limits
☐	☐	☐	2. Cul-de-sac fire access requirements

☐ ☐ ☐   3. Rights of way

☐ ☐ ☐   4. Setbacks and easements

☐ ☐ ☐   5. Line-of-visibility triangles at intersections

Recorded by: _____   Date: _____

Approved by: _____   Date: _____

CHECKLIST 8 STRUCTURAL ENGINEER COORDINATION

Project: _____

Date: _____ Project # _____

ARCHITECTURAL RELATED

Y	N	NA	
☐	☐	☐	1. Structural slab, foundation extents, and waterproofing
☐	☐	☐	2. Basements
☐	☐	☐	3. Footings

LANDSCAPE STRUCTURES

Y	N	NA	
☐	☐	☐	1. Review of structural elements, footings, reinforcement
☐	☐	☐	2. Footings—depth of soil coverage over top of footing
☐	☐	☐	3. Retaining walls
☐	☐	☐	4. Gabions
☐	☐	☐	5. Concrete channels
☐	☐	☐	6. Deck framing plans/overhead trellis structures
☐	☐	☐	7. Pavilions, gazebos, site structures
☐	☐	☐	8. Copy of structural calculations to be submitted to building department; keep for project file
☐	☐	☐	9. Rooftop gardens impact on structure
☐	☐	☐	10. Freeze/thaw design requirements

Recorded by: _____ Date: _____

Approved by: _____ Date: _____

CHECKLIST 9   MECHANICAL AND ELECTRICAL ENGINEER
COORDINATION

Project: _____

Date: _____ Project # _____

MECHANICAL

Y   N   NA

☐   ☐   ☐   1. Water pipes to building

☐   ☐   ☐   2. Air conditioning—location of compressors and ventilation requirements

☐   ☐   ☐   3. Heating

☐   ☐   ☐   4. Ventilation—parking garages, basements

☐   ☐   ☐   5. Irrigation points of connection

☐   ☐   ☐   6. Meters

☐   ☐   ☐   7. Exhausts

ELECTRICAL

Y   N   NA

☐   ☐   ☐   1. Overhead and underground lines/easements

☐   ☐   ☐   2. Electrical points of connection

☐   ☐   ☐   3. Fuseboxes

☐   ☐   ☐   4. Connections for landscape lighting/panels/timer switch

☐   ☐   ☐   5. Transformer locations

☐   ☐   ☐   6. Underground conduit requirements

Recorded by: _____ Date: _____

Approved by: _____ Date: _____

CHECKLIST 10   QUANTITY SURVEYOR COORDINATION

Project: _____

Date: _____ Project # _____

Y	N	NA	
☐	☐	☐	1. Exact extents of landscape budget defined
☐	☐	☐	2. Unit rates/prime cost/provisional sum budgets
☐	☐	☐	3. Items to be included in main contract/builder's work
☐	☐	☐	4. Review of cost estimates/unit pricing
☐	☐	☐	5. Contingencies to be allowed in cost estimates
☐	☐	☐	6. Specification coordination—preliminaries, general requirements, and bid documents
☐	☐	☐	7. Bid review:
☐	☐	☐	a. bid form signatures complete
☐	☐	☐	b. check for computing errors
☐	☐	☐	c. check for exceptions or stipulations
☐	☐	☐	d. check for incomplete submissions
☐	☐	☐	8. Bid/tender report completed

Recorded by: _____ Date: _____

Approved by: _____ Date: _____

CHECKLIST 11   INTERIOR DESIGNER COORDINATION

Project: _____

Date: _____ Project # _____

Y	N	NA	
☐	☐	☐	1. Indoor-outdoor design relationships
☐	☐	☐	2. Interior paving transitions to exterior
☐	☐	☐	3. Material and color themes
☐	☐	☐	4. Textural themes
☐	☐	☐	5. Interior pots/plants
☐	☐	☐	6. Interior planter boxes/drainage/lighting

Recorded by: _____ Date: _____

Approved by: _____ Date: _____

CHECKLIST 12   ARCHITECTURAL LIGHTING CONSULTANT COORDINATION

Project: _____

Date: _____ Project # _____

Y	N	NA	
☐	☐	☐	1. Lighting theme and mood
☐	☐	☐	2. Color of lighting—warm versus cool areas
☐	☐	☐	3. Focal points/spotlights
☐	☐	☐	4. Junction box locations
☐	☐	☐	5. Concealing fixtures
☐	☐	☐	6. Control panel locations
☐	☐	☐	7. Landscape-mounted and building-mounted details
☐	☐	☐	8. Voltage requirements—high and low
☐	☐	☐	9. Photometrics / lighting intensity levels

Recorded by: _____ Date: _____

Approved by: _____ Date: _____

CHECKLIST 13 FOUNTAIN/LAKE/POOL CONSULTANT COORDINATION

Project: _____

Date: _____ Project # _____

FOUNTAINS

Y	N	NA	
☐	☐	☐	1. Equipment requirements/vaults/locations
☐	☐	☐	2. Piping requirements/schematics
☐	☐	☐	3. Filtration system
☐	☐	☐	4. Power requirements/transformers
☐	☐	☐	5. Lighting
☐	☐	☐	6. Maintenance
☐	☐	☐	7. Overflows/connections to drain

LAKES

Y	N	NA	
☐	☐	☐	1. Equipment requirements/vaults/locations
☐	☐	☐	2. Piping requirements/schematics
☐	☐	☐	3. Filtration system
☐	☐	☐	4. Power requirements/transformers
☐	☐	☐	5. Lighting
☐	☐	☐	6. Maintenance
☐	☐	☐	7. Overflows/connections to drain
☐	☐	☐	8. Lake edge design/waterproofing
☐	☐	☐	9. Biological requirements for fish and plants
☐	☐	☐	10. Lake bottom design and levels
☐	☐	☐	11. Slope / pitch of lake bottom for safety

POOLS

Y	N	NA	
☐	☐	☐	1. Equipment requirements/vaults/locations
☐	☐	☐	2. Piping requirements/schematics

☐ ☐ ☐ 3. Filtration system

☐ ☐ ☐ 4. Power requirements/transformers

☐ ☐ ☐ 5. Lighting

☐ ☐ ☐ 6. Maintenance

☐ ☐ ☐ 7. Overflows/connections to drain

☐ ☐ ☐ 8. Coping design—level deck or gutter

☐ ☐ ☐ 9. Accessories—lifeguard station, diving board, ladders

☐ ☐ ☐ 10. Depths required by client

☐ ☐ ☐ 11. ADA requirements for public pools

Recorded by: _____ Date: _____

Approved by: _____ Date: _____

CHECKLIST 14 GEOTECHNICAL AND SOILS AGRNOMIST COORDINATION

Project: _____

Date: _____ Project # _____

Y	N	NA	
☐	☐	☐	1. Geology
☐	☐	☐	2. Soil type, subgrade analysis, and suitability
☐	☐	☐	3. Fertility analysis—sand, silt, clay, loam, humus contents
☐	☐	☐	4. Chemical analysis—PH levels
☐	☐	☐	5. Soil pollution—/suspended solids/septic tank impact
☐	☐	☐	6. Adaptability for reclaimed water usage
☐	☐	☐	7. Recommendations for amendments to support plant material
☐	☐	☐	8. Depth to bedrock
☐	☐	☐	9. Percolation analysis
☐	☐	☐	10. Soil bearing capacity
☐	☐	☐	11. Hazardous or toxic waste discovery

Recorded by: _____ Date: _____

Approved by: _____ Date: _____

CHECKLIST 15   HORTICULTURIST COORDINATION

Project: _____

Date: _____ Project # _____

Y	N	NA	
☐	☐	☐	1. Plant material disease control
☐	☐	☐	2. Tree pruning
☐	☐	☐	3. Large tree transplanting
☐	☐	☐	4. Maintenance specifications
☐	☐	☐	5. Chemical and organic treatments
☐	☐	☐	6. Tree removal methods
☐	☐	☐	7. Compost

Recorded by: _____   Date: _____

Approved by: _____   Date: _____

CHECKLIST 16   DESIGN REQUIREMENTS CHECKLIST

Project: _____

Date: _____ Project # _____

CONCEPT DESIGN

Y	N	NA	
☐	☐	☐	1. Review design on site.
☐	☐	☐	2. Check conformity to codes, ordinances, and deed restrictions.
☐	☐	☐	3. Check compliance with accessibility standards.
☐	☐	☐	4. Check that cost estimate is within budget.
☐	☐	☐	5. Contact agencies about permit and approval requirements.
☐	☐	☐	6. Review contract obligations.
☐	☐	☐	7. Confirm design brief with client.
☐	☐	☐	8. Review the design internally for feedback and suggestions.

DESIGN DEVELOPMENT

Y	N	NA	
☐	☐	☐	1. Concept design theme and program approved by client.
☐	☐	☐	2. Circulation reviewed for conflicts.
☐	☐	☐	3. Color scheme and design works with architectural style.
☐	☐	☐	4. Fire/service access requirements complied with.
☐	☐	☐	5. Design reviewed with any specialists required.
☐	☐	☐	6. Hardscape material samples collected.
☐	☐	☐	7. Plant palette selected.
☐	☐	☐	8. Grading concept/spot elevations/adjacent site levels checked.
☐	☐	☐	9. Lighting concept and material selection completed.
☐	☐	☐	10. Irrigation concept and material selection completed.
☐	☐	☐	11. Current product literature and selection verified.
☐	☐	☐	12. Design meets ADA requirements.
☐	☐	☐	13. Design reviewed for ease of construction and maintenance.
☐	☐	☐	14. Design reviewed for crime prevention and site visibility.

DESIGN PLANNING STANDARDS

Y   **N**   **NA**

- ☐ ☐ ☐   1. Vehicular circulation
- ☐ ☐ ☐   2. Pedestrian circulation
- ☐ ☐ ☐   3. Parks/open space/recreation
- ☐ ☐ ☐   4. Conservation/wetlands
- ☐ ☐ ☐   5. Utility planning—potable water and wastewater
- ☐ ☐ ☐   6. Zoning/land use
- ☐ ☐ ☐   7. Community standards—residential, commercial, industrial
- ☐ ☐ ☐   8. Environmental—soil, slopes, water, vegetation
- ☐ ☐ ☐   9. Maintenance—hardscape and softscape
- ☐ ☐ ☐   10. Stormwater management—runoff, floodplain, water quality, mitigation measures, storage, filtration, percolation

PRIOR TO COMMENCING CONSTRUCTION DOCUMENTS

Y   **N**   **NA**

- ☐ ☐ ☐   1. Review contract obligations.
- ☐ ☐ ☐   2. Review internal design with principal in charge.
- ☐ ☐ ☐   3. Coordinate base sheets with all consultants.
- ☐ ☐ ☐   4. Review consultant coordination checklists.
- ☐ ☐ ☐   5. Obtain client's written approval of design phase.

Recorded by: _____ Date: _____

Approved by: _____ Date: _____

CHECKLIST 17   TYPICAL REPORT OUTLINE

Project: _____

Date: _____ Project # _____

REPORT ORGANIZATION

Y   N   NA

FRONT MATTER

☐ ☐ ☐   1. Cover sheet/report cover graphics

☐ ☐ ☐   2. Table of contents

☐ ☐ ☐   3. Acknowledgments

☐ ☐ ☐   4. Executive summary—purpose, scope, client

CONTENT

☐ ☐ ☐   1. Introduction

☐ ☐ ☐   2. Process, goals, objectives

☐ ☐ ☐   3. Case studies, field research

☐ ☐ ☐   4. Specific report data

☐ ☐ ☐   5. Cost studies

☐ ☐ ☐   6. Analysis/recommendations

☐ ☐ ☐   7. Conclusions

BACK MATTER

☐ ☐ ☐   1. Existing standards/guidelines

☐ ☐ ☐   2. Tables

☐ ☐ ☐   3. Definitions

☐ ☐ ☐   4. Appendix

☐ ☐ ☐   5. Bibliography

REPORT FORMAT

Y	N	NA	
☐	☐	☐	1. Text/typography
☐	☐	☐	2. Graphics—black and white, color, figures, tables
☐	☐	☐	3. Reproduction
☐	☐	☐	4. Binding—hardbound, spiral, cord, etc.
☐	☐	☐	5. Front and back cover stock

Recorded by: _____ Date: _____

Approved by: _____ Date: _____

CHECKLIST 18   LANDSCAPE ASSESSMENT COMPONENTS

Project: _____

Date: _____ Project # _____

GOALS

Y	N	NA	
☐	☐	☐	1. Objectives
☐	☐	☐	2. Problem statement
☐	☐	☐	3. Operational requirements
☐	☐	☐	4. Physical requirements
☐	☐	☐	5. User needs

LAND RESOURCE INVENTORY

Y	N	NA	
☐	☐	☐	1. Water
☐	☐	☐	2. Minerals
☐	☐	☐	3. Vegetation
☐	☐	☐	4. Accessibility
☐	☐	☐	5. Soils
☐	☐	☐	6. Geology
☐	☐	☐	7. Hydrology
☐	☐	☐	8. Slopes
☐	☐	☐	9. Visual analysis
☐	☐	☐	10. Microclimate
☐	☐	☐	11. Structures
☐	☐	☐	12. Acoustics/noise

CLIMATE

Y	N	NA	
☐	☐	☐	1. Sun angles
☐	☐	☐	2. Air quality
☐	☐	☐	3. Temperature
☐	☐	☐	4. Humidity

☐ ☐ ☐   5. Precipitation
☐ ☐ ☐   6. Wind

CULTURE

Y   N   NA

☐ ☐ ☐   1. Archeology
☐ ☐ ☐   2. History
☐ ☐ ☐   3. Landmarks
☐ ☐ ☐   4. Population

BIOLOGICAL

Y   N   NA

☐ ☐ ☐   1. Wildlife
☐ ☐ ☐   2. Insects
☐ ☐ ☐   3. Endangered species
☐ ☐ ☐   4. Habitat

RECLAMATION/CONSERVATION

Y   N   NA

☐ ☐ ☐   1. Vegetation restoration
☐ ☐ ☐   2. Soil analysis
☐ ☐ ☐   3. Erosion control
☐ ☐ ☐   4. Watercourse restoration
☐ ☐ ☐   5. Brownfield development
☐ ☐ ☐   6. Wetland preservation
☐ ☐ ☐   7. Fire ecology
☐ ☐ ☐   8. Conservation value

MCHARG VALUES*

Y   N   NA

☐ ☐ ☐   1. Land value
☐ ☐ ☐   2. Historic value
☐ ☐ ☐   3. Scenic value

☐ ☐ ☐   4. Recreation value

☐ ☐ ☐   5. Water value

☐ ☐ ☐   6. Forest value

☐ ☐ ☐   7. Wildlife value

COSTS

Y   N   NA

☐ ☐ ☐   1. Development

☐ ☐ ☐   2. Permits

☐ ☐ ☐   3. Budget

☐ ☐ ☐   4. Maintenance

☐ ☐ ☐   5. Energy

☐ ☐ ☐   6. Depreciation

ANALYSIS

Y   N   NA

☐ ☐ ☐   1. Opportunities

☐ ☐ ☐   2. Constraints

☐ ☐ ☐   3. Cost/benefit

☐ ☐ ☐   4. Value

☐ ☐ ☐   5. Compatibility

FEASIBILITY

Y   N   NA

☐ ☐ ☐   1. Marketability

☐ ☐ ☐   2. Economics

☐ ☐ ☐   3. Codes and ordinances

☐ ☐ ☐   4. Design

☐ ☐ ☐   5. User group

Recorded by: _____ Date: _____

Approved by: _____ Date: _____

* Ian McHarg, *Design With Nature* (New York: Doubleday/Natural History Press, 1969).

CHECKLIST 19   STORMWATER MANAGEMENT

Project: _____

Date: _____ Project # _____

IDENTIFICATION

Y	N	NA	
☐	☐	☐	1. Flood protection goals
☐	☐	☐	2. Water quality goals
☐	☐	☐	3. Watershed area identified:
☐	☐	☐	a. flow patterns
☐	☐	☐	b. waterways and collection areas
☐	☐	☐	c. aquifers
☐	☐	☐	d. existing drainage systems
☐	☐	☐	4. Climatic information
☐	☐	☐	5. Soil characteristics
☐	☐	☐	6. Groundwater recharge
☐	☐	☐	7. Floodplains
☐	☐	☐	8. Storm year design requirements

ESTIMATION OF RUNOFF

Y	N	NA	
☐	☐	☐	1. Time of concentration (TOC)
☐	☐	☐	a. constant
☐	☐	☐	b. length of travel
☐	☐	☐	c. average slope of flow path
☐	☐	☐	2. Rainfall intensity (I)
☐	☐	☐	a. design storm
☐	☐	☐	b. coefficient for region
☐	☐	☐	3. Peak discharge (Q)
☐	☐	☐	a. runoff coefficient
☐	☐	☐	b. rainfall intensity
☐	☐	☐	c. watershed area

☐ ☐ ☐   4. Water quality volume (WQV)

☐ ☐ ☐   a. design rainfall amount

☐ ☐ ☐   b. percentage of impervious surface

☐ ☐ ☐   c. runoff coefficient

☐ ☐ ☐   5. Time of overland flow (TOF)

☐ ☐ ☐   6. Time of channel flow (TCF)

METHODS

Y   N   NA

☐ ☐ ☐   1. Open systems

☐ ☐ ☐   a. swales

☐ ☐ ☐   b. channels

☐ ☐ ☐   c. culverts

☐ ☐ ☐   2. Closed systems

☐ ☐ ☐   a. storm drains

☐ ☐ ☐   b. storm sewers

☐ ☐ ☐   c. pipes—design and materials

☐ ☐ ☐   d. perforated drains

☐ ☐ ☐   e. head and end walls

☐ ☐ ☐   f. inlets

☐ ☐ ☐   g. catch basins

☐ ☐ ☐   3. Site storage systems

☐ ☐ ☐   a. retention ponds (wet)

☐ ☐ ☐   b. detention ponds (wet/dry)

☐ ☐ ☐   c. sediment basins

☐ ☐ ☐   d. dams

☐ ☐ ☐   4. Filtration

☐ ☐ ☐   a. filtration strips

☐ ☐ ☐   b. sand filters

☐ ☐ ☐   5. Infiltration

☐ ☐ ☐   a. infiltration basins

☐ ☐ ☐   b. recharge trenches

☐ ☐ ☐   c. bioretention ponds

☐ ☐ ☐   d. infiltration beds

☐ ☐ ☐   e. infiltration wells

☐ ☐ ☐   6. Erosion control

☐ ☐ ☐   a. bank treatments—rip-rap/gabions

☐ ☐ ☐   b. slope treatments—benches/geofabric

☐ ☐ ☐   c. vegetation

☐ ☐ ☐   d. porous paving

☐ ☐ ☐   e. filter fencing

ANALYSIS

Y   N   NA

☐ ☐ ☐   1. Cost

☐ ☐ ☐   2. Site clearing mitigation

☐ ☐ ☐   3. Maintenance considerations

VERIFICATION

Y   N   NA

☐ ☐ ☐   1. Coordinate with civil engineer.

☐ ☐ ☐   2. Distribute to client and consultants for review.

Recorded by: _____   Date: _____

Approved by: _____   Date: _____

CHECKLIST 20   URBAN DESIGN COMPONENTS

Project: _____

Date: _____ Project # _____

HIERARCHY

Y	N	NA	
☐	☐	☐	1. Town
☐	☐	☐	2. Community
☐	☐	☐	3. Neighborhood
☐	☐	☐	4. Precinct

FUNCTIONAL STRUCTURE

Y	N	NA	
☐	☐	☐	1. Land use
☐	☐	☐	2. Zoning
☐	☐	☐	3. Jurisdictions—codes

CIRCULATION STRUCTURE

Y	N	NA	
☐	☐	☐	1. Vehicular
☐	☐	☐	2. Pedestrian
☐	☐	☐	3. Path sequence/routes
☐	☐	☐	4. Rail
☐	☐	☐	5. Mass transit
☐	☐	☐	6. Service
☐	☐	☐	7. Parking

SPATIAL STRUCTURE

Y	N	NA	
☐	☐	☐	1. Open space
☐	☐	☐	2. Functional space
☐	☐	☐	3. Building
☐	☐	☐	4. Pattern

☐ ☐ ☐ 5. Activity generators

☐ ☐ ☐ 6. Vistas

☐ ☐ ☐ 7. Mass

☐ ☐ ☐ 8. Cluster

☐ ☐ ☐ 9. Density

MYTHIC STRUCTURE

Y   N   NA

☐ ☐ ☐ 1. Gates

☐ ☐ ☐ 2. Bridges

PERCEPTUAL STRUCTURE

Y   N   NA

☐ ☐ ☐ 1. Lynch elements—nodes, paths, landmarks, edges, districts*

☐ ☐ ☐ 2. Transitional zones

☐ ☐ ☐ 3. Identity

VERNACULAR

Y   N   NA

☐ ☐ ☐ 1. Form

☐ ☐ ☐ 2. Proportion

☐ ☐ ☐ 3. Material

☐ ☐ ☐ 4. Color

☐ ☐ ☐ 5. Texture

MODELS

Y   N   NA

☐ ☐ ☐ 1. Imagery

☐ ☐ ☐ 2. Historical precedents

ANALYSIS

Y	N	NA	
☐	☐	☐	1. Compatibility
☐	☐	☐	2. Suitability
☐	☐	☐	3. Feasibility

Recorded by: _____ Date: _____

Approved by: _____ Date: _____

* Kevin Lynch, *The Image of the City* (Cambridge: MIT Press, 1960).

CHECKLIST 21   ACCESSIBILITY REQUIREMENTS CHECKLIST

Project: _____

Date: _____ Project # _____

ADA Accessibility guidelines may occasionally be updated. This checklist provides a reference to the more common guidelines. Although an effort was made to be as thorough as possible, the list is not all inclusive. Items listed apply to external related guidelines and do not include building interior requirements.

GENERAL

Y	N	NA	
☐	☐	☐	1. Review the accessible route to the building with the architect.
☐	☐	☐	2. Review ADA accessibility guidelines for updates.
☐	☐	☐	3. Provide a letter to the client regarding accessibility requirements that affect the landscape design and budget.
☐	☐	☐	4. If a historic building, check ADA standards section (4.1.7).
☐	☐	☐	5. Is an ADA consultant to be used?

ACCESSIBLE ROUTE

Y	N	NA	
☐	☐	☐	1. Building entry access for accessibility is 50 percent of all but not less than one entry to be accessible. Consult with architect regarding accessible entrance to building. (4.1.3) (4.3.2)
☐	☐	☐	2. Accessible route (at least 36 inches wide) must include a path connecting public sidewalks, public transportation and passenger loading zones. Route must connect different entries for uses on the same site (e.g., strip shopping centers). (4.1.2) (4.1.3)
☐	☐	☐	3. Directional signage is provided at all inaccessible public entrances indicating the location of the accessible entrance. (4.1.3)
☐	☐	☐	4. Wheelchair turning is 60 inches in diameter or a 36-inch by 60-inch three-point turn. (4.2)
☐	☐	☐	5. Curb ramps design requirements are a 1:12 ramp, 36 inches wide. (4.7)
☐	☐	☐	6. Raised islands in crossings along accessible route must be cut level and 48 inches wide. (4.7.11)

WALKWAYS ALONG ACCESSIBLE ROUTE

Y   N   NA

☐ ☐ ☐ 1. Optimum sidewalk width is 60 inches (36 inches minimum; 48 inches in some states). Widen sidewalk to 60 by 60 inches every 200 feet for passing. (4.2) (4.3) (4.3.4)

☐ ☐ ☐ 2. Finish shall have slip-resistant texture. (4.5)

☐ ☐ ☐ 3. There shall be a maximum 2 percent cross-slope perpendicular to direction of travel. (4.3.7)

☐ ☐ ☐ 4. Drain grates shall have maximum 1/2-inch openings. If gratings have elongated openings, place with long opening perpendicular to the direction of travel. (4.5.4)

☐ ☐ ☐ 5. Objects may protrude into a walkway or circulation path a maximum of 4 inches if between 27 and 80 inches above the walking surface. Overhead hazards between 27 and 80 inches must have cane detection element. Watch understair clearances. (4.4)

☐ ☐ ☐ 6. Provide detectable warnings at hazardous vehicular areas and reflecting pools. (4.29.5) (4.29.6)

PARKING

Y   N   NA

☐ ☐ ☐ 1. Check section 4.1.2(5)(a) for the required number of accessible parking spaces. Generally, the quantity is 1 per 25 nonaccessible spaces, then 2 percent when more than 100 spaces. This may vary due to building function. (4.1.2(5)(a))

☐ ☐ ☐ 2. Accessible parking is to be located on shortest possible route of travel to an accessible entrance. (4.6.2)

☐ ☐ ☐ 3. One out of eight accessible spaces is to be van type—96 inches wide and a 96-inch access aisle on the passenger side. Aisle can be shared with another accessible parking space. Include signage for van-type parking. (4.1.2 (5)(b))

☐ ☐ ☐ 4. Passenger loading zones shall be at least 60 inches wide and 20 feet long with curb ramp. Two percent maximum slope in all directions at drop-off. (4.1) (4.6.5) (4.6.6)

☐ ☐ ☐ 5. Parking space maximum slope is 2 percent in all directions. Provide slip-resistant paving and markings per ADA requirements. (4.6.3)

☐ ☐ ☐ 6. Signage for accessible spaces is to be between 5 and 7 feet above pavement. One sign is to be allotted per space with the international symbol of accessibility. (4.6.4)

☐ ☐ ☐   7. Vertical clearance for van accessibility is 8 feet 2 inches. (4.6.5)

☐ ☐ ☐   8. Accessible parking is to be located on the accessible level of the building. (4.1.3)

☐ ☐ ☐   9. No bumper overhangs on sidewalks unless the sidewalk width is widened to accommodate. Pipe bollards or wheel stops may be used. (4.6.3)

☐ ☐ ☐   10. Two accessible spaces can share a common access aisle. (4.6.3)

RAMPS

Y   N   NA

☐ ☐ ☐   1. Slopes at 1:20 (5 percent) or less do not require handrails. Slopes greater than 1:20 are considered ramps. (4.3.7)

☐ ☐ ☐   2. A 1/4-inch maximum rise is allowed with no ramp. A 1/2-inch rise is to be beveled at a 1:2 slope. (4.5.2)

☐ ☐ ☐   3. For a 3-inch rise or less in elevation change, a 1:8 maximum slope is allowed. (This may require a variance in some states.) (4.1.6(3))

☐ ☐ ☐   4. For curb ramps with a 6-inch rise, a 1:10 to 1:12 maximum slope is allowed. Ramps to have 5-foot landings top and bottom and be at least 3 feet wide. Sides to slope at 1:10 maximum. Adjoining sidewalk and road slope not to be greater than 1:20. (4.7) Provide detectible warning device. (4.29.2) (Slope variations may require a variance in some states).

☐ ☐ ☐   5. Ramps slope at 1:12 maximum. The maximum run for any rise is 30 feet. (4.8)

☐ ☐ ☐   6. Ramps shall have landings at the top, bottom, and every 30 feet of run. Landings shall be as wide as the ramp unless there is a change of direction (see #7 below). Landing length shall be 60 inches. (4.8.4)

☐ ☐ ☐   7. Ramp changes in direction require a 60 by 60-inch landing. (4.8.4)

☐ ☐ ☐   8. Handrails are required for all ramps and slopes exceeding 1:20 (5 percent) or 6-inch rise. Rails are to be on both sides at 36 inches apart and continuous. Rail diameter is a maximum of 2 inches. Handrail height at 34 to 38 inches above paved surface. Extend handrails 12 inches beyond top and bottom of ramp. Clear space between handrail and wall is 1-1/2 inches. (4.8.5) (4.26)

☐ ☐ ☐   9. The maximum length of a ramp without a handrail is 6 feet. (4.8.5)

☐ ☐ ☐   10. Platform lifts have special ADA requirements. (4.1.3) (4.11)

DOORS (AT BUILDING ENTRY ALONG ACCESSIBLE ROUTE)

Y   N   NA

☐   ☐   ☐   1. Front approach pull-type doors are to have a 60-inch clearance away from door or building wall on the latch side. Strike side clearance is 18 inches minimum. (4.13)

☐   ☐   ☐   2. Front approach push-type doors are to have a 48-inch clearance from door or building wall. A 12-inch minimum width is required on the door handle side if door has both a closer and a latch. (4.13)

☐   ☐   ☐   3. The minimum clear door width is 32 inches. (4.13)

☐   ☐   ☐   4. The unobstructed forward and side reach is 15 inches minimum to 48 inches maximum, with 36 to 42 inches optimum. (4.13) (New ADA standards have one reach range of 48 inches maximum, but current standards allow 54 inches for side approach).

DRINKING FOUNTAINS

Y   N   NA

☐   ☐   ☐   1. A total of 50 percent but not less than one of the total number of drinking fountains are to be a wheelchair-accessible type. Provide one higher unit for stooping disabilities. (4.1.3(10))

☐   ☐   ☐   2. The wheelchair spout is to be at a height of 36 inches. (4.15)

☐   ☐   ☐   3. Wall mounted drink fountains shall have clear knee space. (4.15.5)

HANDRAILS

Y   N   NA

☐   ☐   ☐   1. Extend the handrail past stairs one tread width plus 12 inches on the bottom and 12 inches width on the top. Round top rail smooth. Extension shall be parallel with the landing level. (4.9.4)

☐   ☐   ☐   2. Optimum size of the handrail is 1-1/2 inches. (4.26)

☐   ☐   ☐   3. Spacing between the rail and the wall should be exactly 1-1/2 inches. (4.9.4)

☐   ☐   ☐   4. Handrail height should be between 34 and 38 inches above paved surface. (4.9.4)

STEPS

Y   N   NA

☐   ☐   ☐   1. Provide handrails at both sides of stairs if three or more risers. (4.9.4)

☐   ☐   ☐   2. Stair nosing cannot protrude more than 1-1/2 inches. (4.9.3)

☐   ☐   ☐   3. Minimum tread width is 11 inches. (4.9.2)

PUBLIC TELEPHONES

Y	N	NA	
☐	☐	☐	1. For every four or more telephones, one must be a text type (TTY) phone. TTY phone must have a shelf and electrical outlet. (4.1.3(17))
☐	☐	☐	2. Telephone to have a 30 by 48-inch clear frontage for wheelchair access. (4.31.2)
☐	☐	☐	3. Maximum 48-inch mounting height to highest operable part. (4.31.2)
☐	☐	☐	4. For wall-mounted phones, conform to maximum 27 inches in height from floor for cane detector. (4.4)

SIGNAGE

Y	N	NA	
☐	☐	☐	1. When accessible signage is required, use international symbol of accessibility. (4.30)
☐	☐	☐	2. Use contrasting background and letters. (4.30.5)

SEATING

Y	N	NA	
☐	☐	☐	1. Knee clearances—27 inches high, 30 inches wide, 19 inches deep. (4.32.3)
☐	☐	☐	2. Table heights—between 28 and 34 inches from ground level. (4.32.4)
☐	☐	☐	3. Allow 30 by 48 inches of wheelchair pull-up space to table or adjacent seating. (4.32)

MISCELLANEOUS

Y	N	NA	
☐	☐	☐	1. Fountains and reflecting pools to have a railing, wall, curb, or detectable warning device. (4.29.6)

Recorded by: _____   Date: _____

Approved by: _____   Date: _____

CHECKLIST 22   BASE SHEET CHECKLIST

Project: _____

Date: _____ Project # _____

COVER SHEET

Y	N	NA	
☐	☐	☐	1. Project name and location
☐	☐	☐	2. Title block and signature block
☐	☐	☐	3. List of drawings
☐	☐	☐	4. Vicinity map/regional map/key map
☐	☐	☐	5. Abbreviation listing
☐	☐	☐	6. Agency approval space

STANDARD SHEET INFORMATION

Y	N	NA	
☐	☐	☐	1. Base sheet size and scale consistent with agency submittal requirements.
☐	☐	☐	2. Title block including sheet title, company name, job number, sheet number, drawn by and checked by box, registration seal box, revision block
☐	☐	☐	3. Scale/date/north arrow
☐	☐	☐	4. Key plan/matchlines
☐	☐	☐	5. Items noted N.I.C. or BY OTHERS.

SITE INFORMATION

Y	N	NA	
☐	☐	☐	1. Boundary survey
☐	☐	☐	2. Right-of-way lines/setbacks
☐	☐	☐	3. Topography—existing spot elevations/contours/boundary elevations
☐	☐	☐	4. Limit of work lines
☐	☐	☐	5. Matchlines
☐	☐	☐	6. Address/street names
☐	☐	☐	7. Tract number/Lot number
☐	☐	☐	8. Street curbs, curb cuts, driveway turning radius

☐ ☐ ☐   9. Public sidewalks and required sidewalks

☐ ☐ ☐   10. Existing features to remain

☐ ☐ ☐   11. Existing trees and vegetation

☐ ☐ ☐   12. Signage

☐ ☐ ☐   13. Line-of-sight triangles at intersections and drives

☐ ☐ ☐   14. Demarcate areas in 100-year floodplain

☐ ☐ ☐   15. Existing site amenities/features

☐ ☐ ☐   16. Parking areas

☐ ☐ ☐   17. Roadway classifications/street names/curb and gutter

☐ ☐ ☐   18. Existing drainage elements

ARCHITECTURAL INFORMATION

Y   N   NA

☐ ☐ ☐   1. Building footprint

☐ ☐ ☐   2. Building overhangs

☐ ☐ ☐   3. Doors and windows

☐ ☐ ☐   4. Finish floor elevations

☐ ☐ ☐   5. Building numbers

☐ ☐ ☐   6. Service areas

☐ ☐ ☐   7. Other structures

UTILITY INFORMATION

Y   N   NA

☐ ☐ ☐   1. Easements—water, gas, electric, storm and sanitary sewers, telephone, cable

☐ ☐ ☐   2. Vaults, meters, manholes, culverts

☐ ☐ ☐   3. Light poles, transformers

☐ ☐ ☐   4. Hydrants

☐ ☐ ☐   5. Drainage channels/swales

VERIFICATION

Y	N	NA	
☐	☐	☐	1. Overlay consultant drawings to verify base sheet layout.
☐	☐	☐	2. Distribute base sheet to other consultants for review prior to proceeding with drawings.
☐	☐	☐	3. Complete, sign, and file checklist.

Recorded by: _____   Date: _____

Approved by: _____   Date: _____

CHECKLIST 23   DEMOLITION PLAN CHECKLIST

Project: _____

Date: _____ Project # _____

SHEET INFORMATION

Y	N	NA	
☐	☐	☐	1. Base sheet information, correctly displayed
☐	☐	☐	2. Limit of work/matchlines/key map
☐	☐	☐	3. Note items N.I.C. or BY OTHERS.
☐	☐	☐	4. Graphic symbols/legend
☐	☐	☐	5. Labels/callouts
☐	☐	☐	6. Dimensions
☐	☐	☐	7. General demolition notes

SITE INFORMATION

Y	N	NA	
☐	☐	☐	1. Overlay construction plan to verify items to be demolished.
☐	☐	☐	2. Underground utilities—identify if they are to be retained, filled, removed, or abandoned.
☐	☐	☐	3. Indicate hoardings to be erected.
☐	☐	☐	4. Trees to be removed, sizes, and locations—clarify if roots are to be removed.
☐	☐	☐	5. Trees to remain—protection measures to be taken and no grading within driplines of canopy; pruning requirements
☐	☐	☐	6. Site clearing and grubbing
☐	☐	☐	7. Sod stripping
☐	☐	☐	8. Soil stabilization
☐	☐	☐	9. Temporary installations/site measures—erosion control, site office location, construction parking, and material storage

CLAUSES

Y	N	NA	
☐	☐	☐	1. Toxic waste clause indicating that "Landscape architect has no responsibility for dealing with hazardous substances that may be found during the course of demolition or site work."
☐	☐	☐	2. Identify if rubble can be used as backfill.
☐	☐	☐	3. Clause indicating that "Landscape architect is not responsible for any items that may be discovered on site during demolition or construction that were not previously indicated on the surveys or information provided."

VERIFICATION

Y	N	NA	
☐	☐	☐	1. Verify demolition of utilities with owner and other consultants.
☐	☐	☐	2. Verify demolition of structures with owner and architect.
☐	☐	☐	3. Complete, sign, and file checklist.
☐	☐	☐	4. Place landscape architect seal on drawing.

Recorded by: _____   Date: _____

Approved by: _____   Date: _____

CHECKLIST 24   CONSTRUCTION PLAN CHECKLIST

Project: _____

Date: _____ Project # _____

SHEET INFORMATION

Y	N	NA	
☐	☐	☐	1. Base sheet information correctly reflected.
☐	☐	☐	2. Existing conditions shown and indicated TO REMAIN.
☐	☐	☐	3. Note items N.I.C. and BY OTHERS. Indicate who will install and guarantee.
☐	☐	☐	4. Construction legend, callouts, and section lines indicated.
☐	☐	☐	5. Schedules reflect materials, colors, textures, and reference to construction details.
☐	☐	☐	6. General construction notes and any special requirements.

LAYOUT INFORMATION

Y	N	NA	
☐	☐	☐	1. All construction items properly referenced.
☐	☐	☐	2. Section lines shown.
☐	☐	☐	3. Dimensions shown with point of beginning and confirm they match consultant drawings. Control points indicated. GIS coordinates shown.
☐	☐	☐	4. Service access requirements—fire, maintenance, trash, delivery, mail.
☐	☐	☐	5. Indicate accessible parking and route to building. Crosswalks and ramps to be clearly marked.
☐	☐	☐	6. Water tap points and electric meter.
☐	☐	☐	7. Specified products to include item type, model number, color, and supplier.
☐	☐	☐	8. Sleeves indicated for drainage pipe, irrigation pipe, and electrical conduit.
☐	☐	☐	9. Fences and wall heights meet code requirements.
☐	☐	☐	10. Expansion and control joints shown.
☐	☐	☐	11. Roadway design speed, sight distances, alignment, and grading.
☐	☐	☐	12. Radius at roadway and driveway corners conform to codes.
☐	☐	☐	13. Existing and proposed utilities shown.

☐ ☐ ☐ 14. Recreational facilities conform to standards.

☐ ☐ ☐ 15. Exterior pavement is nonslip.

☐ ☐ ☐ 16. Ensure that "or equal" items actually have an equal.

☐ ☐ ☐ 17. Indicate drainage elements and key to grading plan.

☐ ☐ ☐ 18. Detail reference to paving transitions.

☐ ☐ ☐ 19. Driveway widths, aprons, and radii conform to codes.

☐ ☐ ☐ 20. Handrails and railings shown.

AGENCY REQUIREMENTS

Y   N   NA

☐ ☐ ☐ 1. Recheck compliance to land use ordinances, building codes, deed restrictions, health codes, ADA requirements, OSHA, and local, city, and county codes.

☐ ☐ ☐ 2. Seal and submit for agency approvals.

☐ ☐ ☐ 3. Signage requirements meet codes.

VERIFICATION

Y   N   NA

☐ ☐ ☐ 1. Distribute to owner and consultants for review and comment.

☐ ☐ ☐ 2. Complete, sign, and file checklist.

Recorded by: _____ Date: _____

Approved by: _____ Date: _____

CHECKLIST 25   CONSTRUCTION DETAILS CHECKLIST

Project: _____

Date: _____ Project # _____

SHEET INFORMATION

Y	N	NA	
☐	☐	☐	1. Determine detail format—drawing sheet size or 8-1/2 by 11 inches (A4) or 11 by 17 inches (A3).
☐	☐	☐	2. Cover sheet and list of details.

DETAIL INFORMATION

Y	N	NA	
☐	☐	☐	1. Demolition details
☐	☐	☐	2. Construction details
☐	☐	☐	3. Grading details
☐	☐	☐	4. Planting details
☐	☐	☐	5. Lighting details
☐	☐	☐	6. Irrigation details
☐	☐	☐	7. Details conform to approved design concept.
☐	☐	☐	8. Details referenced back to plans.
☐	☐	☐	9. Finishes, colors, and textures indicated.
☐	☐	☐	10. Dimensions
☐	☐	☐	11. References match architecture finishes.
☐	☐	☐	12. Connections at architecture thresholds
☐	☐	☐	13. Drainage elements referenced to grading plan.
☐	☐	☐	14. Check wall footings against hardscape and softscape.
☐	☐	☐	15. Tie-ins to existing elements shown.
☐	☐	☐	16. Thermal and moisture protection indicated.
☐	☐	☐	17. Painting and coatings referenced.
☐	☐	☐	18. Drawings and details of subconsultants included in set.

VERIFICATION

Y	N	NA	
☐	☐	☐	1. Structural details to be reviewed and approved by engineer and calculations to be filed.
☐	☐	☐	2. Distribute to owner and consultants for review and comment.
☐	☐	☐	3. Complete, sign, and file checklist.
☐	☐	☐	4. Landscape architect seal.

Recorded by: _____ Date: _____

Approved by: _____ Date: _____

CHECKLIST 26   GRADING PLAN CHECKLIST

Project: _____

Date: _____ Project # _____

SHEET INFORMATION

Y	N	NA	
☐	☐	☐	1. Base sheet information correctly reflected.
☐	☐	☐	2. Grading legend and notes shown.
☐	☐	☐	3. Note items N.I.C. and BY OTHERS.

GRADING INFORMATION

Y	N	NA	
☐	☐	☐	1. Existing contours. Meet existing grade at property line. Datum elevations shown.
☐	☐	☐	2. Proposed contours shown.
☐	☐	☐	3. Spot elevations and fine grading to show top and bottom of walls, steps, and ramps.
☐	☐	☐	4. Finish floor elevations of all structures and pad grades. Proposed gradelevels at building corners. Allow for basement windows.
☐	☐	☐	5. Top of fences and rails.
☐	☐	☐	6. Step risers and treads indicated.
☐	☐	☐	7. Paved areas sloped at 1 percent minimum. Flow arrows shown.
☐	☐	☐	8. Planting areas slope at 2 percent minimum. Swale flow arrows shown.
☐	☐	☐	9. Slopes greater than 3:1 cannot be mowed.
☐	☐	☐	10. Swale flow directions and high/low points shown.
☐	☐	☐	11. Check sport facility grading with code requirements.
☐	☐	☐	12. No grading within driplines of existing trees.
☐	☐	☐	13. Flat benches at top and bottom of slopes.
☐	☐	☐	14. Planting beds adjacent to walkways drain away from walk.
☐	☐	☐	15. Cut and fill calculations estimated.
☐	☐	☐	16. Slopes on walks and parking along accessible route conform to ADA guidelines.
☐	☐	☐	17. Excavation and backfill material relates to specifications.

☐ ☐ ☐   18. Soil stabilization methods shown.

☐ ☐ ☐   19. Drainage onto adjacent property conforms to codes.

☐ ☐ ☐   20. Driveways maximum 10 percent slope.

☐ ☐ ☐   21. Parking areas maximum 3 percent slope.

☐ ☐ ☐   22. Runoff drainage from large paved areas is mitigated.

☐ ☐ ☐   23. Positive flow away from buildings.

DRAINAGE INFORMATION

Y   N   NA

☐ ☐ ☐   1. Catch basins shown with size, invert elevation, and detail reference.

☐ ☐ ☐   2. Deck drains shown with size, invert elevation, and detail reference.

☐ ☐ ☐   3. Points of connection of drain lines shown.

☐ ☐ ☐   4. French/perforated subsurface drain pipe shown with size, inverts, and detail reference.

☐ ☐ ☐   5. Piping inverts shown at ends and corners. Drain lines sloped at 0.5 percent minimum and pipe sizes indicated.

☐ ☐ ☐   6. Planter box drains and pipe connections shown with reference to details.

☐ ☐ ☐   7. Manhole rim and invert elevations shown.

☐ ☐ ☐   8. Minimum 12-inch soil cover over pipes—24 inches optimum.

☐ ☐ ☐   9. Fountain/pool drains shown

☐ ☐ ☐   10. Design of open channels, culverts, and storm drainage to be coordinated with engineer.

☐ ☐ ☐   11. Ponds, culverts, and detention basins consulted with engineer.

☐ ☐ ☐   12. Floodplain indicated.

☐ ☐ ☐   13. Waterproofing specified.

VERIFICATION

Y   N   NA

☐ ☐ ☐   1. Distribute to owner and consultants for review and comment.

☐ ☐ ☐   2. Complete, sign, and file checklist.

☐ ☐ ☐   3. Landscape architect seal.

Recorded by: _____   Date: _____

Approved by: _____   Date: _____

CHECKLIST 27 PLANTING PLAN CHECKLIST

Project: _____

Date: _____ Project # _____

SHEET INFORMATION

Y	N	NA	
☐	☐	☐	1. Base sheet correctly reflected.
☐	☐	☐	2. Note items N.I.C. and BY OTHERS.
☐	☐	☐	3. Planting notes.
☐	☐	☐	4. Planting legend including botanical and common names, size, height, spread, spacing, remarks, staking method, detail reference.

PLANTING DESIGN

Y	N	NA	
☐	☐	☐	1. Note existing trees and shrubs to remain undisturbed.
☐	☐	☐	2. Plant palette confirmed by owner.
☐	☐	☐	3. Plant material conforms to soils agronomy report.
☐	☐	☐	4. Correct sun/shade exposures.
☐	☐	☐	5. Indicate areas of slope stabilization/geofabric and reference to details. Relate to grading plan.
☐	☐	☐	6. Planter/pot drainage and reference to details.
☐	☐	☐	7. Confirm plant material availability before specifying and indicate sources for specimen plant material.
☐	☐	☐	8. Verify root box/ball will fit in pit size provided.
☐	☐	☐	9. Show planters, pots, and hanging baskets. Provide legend and manufacturer and supplier information.
☐	☐	☐	10. Details for water plants—bed type, pots, underwater or floating type. Indicate submersible depth.
☐	☐	☐	11. Type of bed edging and detail.
☐	☐	☐	12. Grass type and installation method (seed, hydromulch, sod). Indicate acceptable planting time/season for grasses.
☐	☐	☐	13. Vine locations and wall espalier detail.
☐	☐	☐	14. Indicate root barriers for trees adjacent to pavement.
☐	☐	☐	15. Indicate trees to be single- or multi-trunk.

☐ ☐ ☐   16. Annual color change-outs per season.

☐ ☐ ☐   17. Reference soil treatment and mulching to specifications.

☐ ☐ ☐   18. Coordinate planting and lighting fixtures.

☐ ☐ ☐   19. Review planting with accessible route to ensure that plants with thorns, drooping branches, seed pods, cones, nuts, and acorns, are away from access paths.

☐ ☐ ☐   20. Indicate trunk protection measures.

☐ ☐ ☐   21. Ensure tree placement does not conflict with underground or overhead utilities.

☐ ☐ ☐   22. Planting design for fire mitigation if required.

☐ ☐ ☐   23. Plants tolerant to adverse site conditions.

☐ ☐ ☐   24. Use of toxic plants reviewed with client before specifying.

☐ ☐ ☐   25. Special plant requirements mentioned in notes.

☐ ☐ ☐   26. Metal edging kept away from high-traffic areas.

☐ ☐ ☐   27. Indicate no tree staking adjacent to pedestrian traffic areas.

MAINTENANCE

Y   N   NA

☐ ☐ ☐   1. Slopes with grass do not exceed 3:1.

☐ ☐ ☐   2. Verify clearance between trees and beds for mowing access.

☐ ☐ ☐   3. No turf in deep shade or under large tree canopies.

☐ ☐ ☐   4. Special pruning requirements noted on plans.

☐ ☐ ☐   5. Specify interior plants to be acclimated.

VERIFICATION

Y   N   NA

☐ ☐ ☐   1. Send to owner for review and comment.

☐ ☐ ☐   2. Complete, sign, and file checklist.

☐ ☐ ☐   3. Place landscape architect seal.

Recorded by: _____   Date: _____

Approved by: _____   Date: _____

CHECKLIST 28   INTERIOR PLANTING PLAN CHECKLIST

Project: _____

Date: _____ Project # _____

SHEET INFORMATION

Y	N	NA	
☐	☐	☐	1. Base sheet correctly reflected.
☐	☐	☐	2. Note items N.I.C. and BY OTHERS.
☐	☐	☐	3. Planting notes.
☐	☐	☐	4. Planting legend including botanical and common names, size, height, spread, spacing, remarks, staking method, detail reference.

PLANTING DESIGN

Y	N	NA	
☐	☐	☐	1. Verify light orientation, intensity, duration, and quality. Indicate supplemental light sources required.
☐	☐	☐	2. Plant palette confirmed by owner.
☐	☐	☐	3. Plant selection for building temperature and low humidity.
☐	☐	☐	4. Indicate drip irrigation system. If hand watering, provide maintenance guidelines.
☐	☐	☐	5. Check building ventilation system for air blowing onto plants.
☐	☐	☐	6. Planter/pot drainage and reference to details.
☐	☐	☐	7. Confirm plant material availability before specifying and indicate sources for specimen plant material.
☐	☐	☐	8. Planter drainage system adequate.
☐	☐	☐	9. Show planters, pots, and hanging baskets. Provide legend and manufacturer and supplier information.
☐	☐	☐	10. Plant mix for interior pots added to specifications.
☐	☐	☐	11. Indicate trees to be single- or multi-trunk.
☐	☐	☐	12. Specify interior plants to be acclimated.

VERIFICATION

Y	N	NA	
☐	☐	☐	1. Send to owner for review and comment.
☐	☐	☐	2. Complete, sign, and file checklist.
☐	☐	☐	3. Place landscape architect seal.

Recorded by: _____   Date: _____

Approved by: _____   Date: _____

CHECKLIST 29 LIGHTING PLAN CHECKLIST

Project: _____

Date: _____ Project # _____

SHEET INFORMATION

Y	N	NA	
☐	☐	☐	1. Base sheet correctly reflected.
☐	☐	☐	2. Note items N.I.C. and BY OTHERS.
☐	☐	☐	3. Lighting notes.
☐	☐	☐	4. Lighting legend including fixture, manufacturer, model number, lamp color, wattage, pole type, detail reference.

LIGHTING DESIGN

Y	N	NA	
☐	☐	☐	1. Electrical power source, meter, switches, panel location, timers.
☐	☐	☐	2. Installation details, mounting, and footings.
☐	☐	☐	3. Verify all fixtures are UL-exterior approved.
☐	☐	☐	4. File calculations for foot-candles and photometric charts.
☐	☐	☐	5. Indicate sleeve locations for conduit.
☐	☐	☐	6. Parking lot poles located between stalls. Ensure space for car bumpers to not hit poles.
☐	☐	☐	7. Light pole footings details.
☐	☐	☐	8. Indicate outdoor electrical outlets (waterproof type).
☐	☐	☐	9. Verify step lights included.
☐	☐	☐	10. Show low-voltage and high-voltage systems.
☐	☐	☐	11. Underwater lights for pools and fountains shown with proper grounding.
☐	☐	☐	12. Coordinate light locations with planting plan.
☐	☐	☐	13. Review to ensure no glare onto roadways and parking lots.
☐	☐	☐	14. Review design of lamp colors on objects:
☐	☐	☐	a. No mercury vapor on people.
☐	☐	☐	b. Minimize yellow-orange sodium on plants.
☐	☐	☐	c. Warm light best on architectural elements.
☐	☐	☐	d. Cool light best on plants.

☐ ☐ ☐   15. Signage lighting indicated.

☐ ☐ ☐   16. Review illumination levels against codes and standards.

VERIFICATION

Y   **N**   **NA**

☐ ☐ ☐   1. Review pole spacing and installation requirements with manufacturer.

☐ ☐ ☐   2. Coordinate power sources with electrical engineer.

☐ ☐ ☐   3. Check code compliance.

☐ ☐ ☐   4. Send to owner and consultants for review and comment.

☐ ☐ ☐   5. Complete, sign, and file checklist.

☐ ☐ ☐   6. Place landscape architect seal.

Recorded by: _____ Date: _____

Approved by: _____ Date: _____

CHECKLIST 30   IRRIGATION PLAN CHECKLIST

Project: _____

Date: _____ Project # _____

SHEET INFORMATION

Y	N	NA	
☐	☐	☐	1. Base sheet correctly reflected.
☐	☐	☐	2. Note items N.I.C. and BY OTHERS.
☐	☐	☐	3. Irrigation notes.
☐	☐	☐	4. Irrigation legend.
☐	☐	☐	5. Watering schedule on plans and in specifications.

IRRIGATION DESIGN

Y	N	NA	
☐	☐	☐	1. Indicate P.O.C./water meter—size and pressure.
☐	☐	☐	2. Indicate power for controller.
☐	☐	☐	3. Backflow prevention device meets agency requirements and not in a prominent visual location.
☐	☐	☐	4. Check head coverage and spacing for overlapping of spray.
☐	☐	☐	5. Soil considerations.
☐	☐	☐	6. Wind considerations.
☐	☐	☐	7. Gate valves shown.
☐	☐	☐	8. Pipe sizes indicated.
☐	☐	☐	9. Controller location indicated.
☐	☐	☐	10. Drip irrigation provisions for pottery and planter boxes.
☐	☐	☐	11. Hose bibs/quick couplers shown.
☐	☐	☐	12. No spray heads below tree grates.
☐	☐	☐	13. No irrigation over walkways/driveways/roads.
☐	☐	☐	14. Recheck planting types, native areas, drought-tolerant plants.
☐	☐	☐	15. Water source—reclaimed/effluent water use requires special permits.
☐	☐	☐	16. Piping avoids driplines of existing trees.

VERIFICATION

Y	N	NA	
☐	☐	☐	1. Send to owner and consultants for review and comment.
☐	☐	☐	2. Complete, sign, and file checklist.
☐	☐	☐	3. Place landscape architect seal.

Recorded by: _____ Date: _____

Approved by: _____ Date: _____

CHECKLIST 31   SPECIALTY ITEMS: TENNIS COURTS

Project: _____

Date: _____ Project # _____

DESIGN ISSUES

Y	N	NA	
☐	☐	☐	1. Verify size of court meets with class of play required by owner.
☐	☐	☐	2. Specify court paving (asphalt, asphaltic concrete, concrete, clay, grass, special surfacing, colors).
☐	☐	☐	3. Court layout in north-south direction (22 degrees off N maximum).
☐	☐	☐	4. Confirm other amenities (drinking fountains, speakers, scoreboard, time clock, audience seating, player seating, umpire seat).
☐	☐	☐	5. Confirm drainage per agency requirements.
☐	☐	☐	6. Drainage at 0.5–1 percent cross-slope and 0.5 percent end to end for hard surfaces or 1 percent for clay and grass. High point not at net.
☐	☐	☐	7. Net and post design.
☐	☐	☐	8. Connection details for paving, lighting, net posts, and fencing.
☐	☐	☐	9. Provide waterproofing if on rooftop and coordinate with architect.
☐	☐	☐	10. Signage requirements.
☐	☐	☐	11. Shaded seating area for waiting.

LIGHTING

Y	N	NA	
☐	☐	☐	1. Confirm lights meet standards for type of court (championship or recreational).
☐	☐	☐	2. Light spacing and heights per manufacturers recommendations.
☐	☐	☐	3. Confirm if timer or switch.
☐	☐	☐	4. Safety lighting provided when court lights are off.

FENCING

Y	N	NA	
☐	☐	☐	1. Determine height (10–12 feet) and check that material (vinyl coated, mesh, chain link) meets owner requirements.
☐	☐	☐	2. Confirm if windscreen is required. Check color.
☐	☐	☐	3. Fence gate and maintenance access.

Recorded by: _____ Date: _____

Approved by: _____ Date: _____

CHECKLIST 32   SPECIALTY ITEMS: SWIMMING POOLS

Project: _____

Date: _____ Project # _____

POOL EQUIPMENT

Y   N   NA

☐   ☐   ☐   1. Verify agency requirements for setback of equipment and pool edges.

☐   ☐   ☐   2. Verify health department and local agency approval of selection and layout.

☐   ☐   ☐   3. Review equipment with pool contractor and engineer.

☐   ☐   ☐   4. Verify equipment fits in equipment room provided and space is allocated for chemicals, hooks, tubes, etc.

☐   ☐   ☐   5. Allocate lead time for equipment delivery.

☐   ☐   ☐   6. Control panel location for switches, timer and panel box.

☐   ☐   ☐   7. Pool heater requirements.

DESIGN

Y   N   NA

☐   ☐   ☐   1. Layout meets local codes for clear deck area, spa distance from pool, artificial rock into pool, filtration system, and type of gutter system.

☐   ☐   ☐   2. Gutter or level deck system.

☐   ☐   ☐   3. Indicate pool depths, steps, diving board, ladders, and lifeguard tower.

☐   ☐   ☐   4. Lifesaving equipment per code requirements.

☐   ☐   ☐   5. Pool perimeter fence height, location, and design per codes. Pool gate self-closing /self-latching requirements.

☐   ☐   ☐   6. Details of pool edge, coping, gutter, weirs, and finishes.

☐   ☐   ☐   7. Material and color of pool surface approved by health department (tile, plaster, GFRC, gunite).

☐   ☐   ☐   8. Deck to have nonslip surface and be light in color.

☐   ☐   ☐   9. Spa information including timer switch, jets and nozzles, bench design, and heater controls.

☐   ☐   ☐   10. Review shop drawings from pool contractor, including automatic water feed/regulator, waterproof membrane, water stops, pipe penetrations, overflows, drains, filters, pumps, lighting, and furnishings.

☐ ☐ ☐   11. Lighting for pools has a minimum 2-inch water cover over fixture. All
          fixtures grounded.

☐ ☐ ☐   12. Signage for public pool safety.

☐ ☐ ☐   13. Pool cover detail, if applicable.

☐ ☐ ☐   14. Review tree types existing and specified next to pool.

☐ ☐ ☐   15. Public pool requirements for accessibility or any special apparatus
          required.

☐ ☐ ☐   16. Adjacent surfaces slope away from pool.

☐ ☐ ☐   17. Drains indicated.

Recorded by: _____   Date: _____

Approved by: _____   Date: _____

CHECKLIST 33 SPECIALTY ITEMS: WATER FEATURES

Project: _____

Date: _____ Project # _____

EQUIPMENT

Y	N	NA	
☐	☐	☐	1. Verify agency requirements for setback of equipment.
☐	☐	☐	2. Review equipment with pool contractor and engineer.
☐	☐	☐	3. Verify equipment fits in equipment room provided and sufficient space allocated for chemicals, hooks, tubes, etc.
☐	☐	☐	4. Allocate lead time for equipment delivery.
☐	☐	☐	5. Control panel location for switches, timer, and panel box.
☐	☐	☐	6. Pump type (submersible or centrifugal).
☐	☐	☐	7. Sump details, sections, and access.
☐	☐	☐	8. Maintenance manual provided.

FOUNTAIN AND WEIR DESIGN

Y	N	NA	
☐	☐	☐	1. Details of pool edge, coping, gutter, weirs, and finishes.
☐	☐	☐	2. Review shop drawings of contractor, including auto water feed/regulator, waterproof membrane, water stops, pipe penetrations, overflows, drains, filters, pumps, lighting, furnishings, wind sensors, timers, flow switches, level sensors.
☐	☐	☐	3. Underwater lighting has a minimum of 2 inches water cover above top of fixture. Underwater lighting is grounded.
☐	☐	☐	4. Water level control devices.
☐	☐	☐	5. Indicate length of weirs, depth of water over weir, flow rate, head, power requirements, and volume.
☐	☐	☐	6. Coordinate nozzles and jets with supplier and contractor.
☐	☐	☐	7. Review design to ensure desired effects.
☐	☐	☐	8. Allow for wind on vertical jets. Pool width 2 times jet height.
☐	☐	☐	9. Minimum 18 inches depth to deter algae growth.

LAKE DESIGN

Y	N	NA	
☐	☐	☐	1. Coordinate lake filtration system with specialist (biofilters, ozone, equipment, fish and plant adaptability).
☐	☐	☐	2. Indicate lake bottom structure (concrete, shotcrete, liner, gunite, waterproofing).
☐	☐	☐	3. Review lake edge design. Maximum 3:1 slope at edge.
☐	☐	☐	4. Review shop drawings of pool contractor, including auto water feed/regulator, waterproof membrane, water stops, pipe penetrations, overflows, drains, filters, pumps, lighting, and furnishings.
☐	☐	☐	5. Lighting for pools has a minimum of 2 inches water cover above top of fixture. Underwater lighting is grounded.
☐	☐	☐	6. Allow for shallow area for the first 5 feet of lake with gradual slope in case of children falling into water.
☐	☐	☐	7. Provide shallow swale before lake edge to catch silt and fertilizers from draining into lake.
☐	☐	☐	8. Water plant details.
☐	☐	☐	9. Lake consultant to provide maintenance manual.
☐	☐	☐	10. Lake depth of 8–10 feet minimum required for aquatic life.
☐	☐	☐	11. Minimize fertilizer runoff into lake.
☐	☐	☐	12. Check codes for perimeter fence requirements.
☐	☐	☐	13. Show and detail drains.

Recorded by: _____ Date: _____

Approved by: _____ Date: _____

CHECKLIST 34   SPECIALTY ITEMS: CHILDREN'S PLAYGROUNDS

Project: _____

Date: _____ Project # _____

Y	N	NA	
☐	☐	☐	1. Playground equipment specified corresponds to intended user age group. Provide adequate spacing between equipment.
☐	☐	☐	2. Review all play equipment fall zones with manufacturer and indicate fall zone dimensions on plan.
☐	☐	☐	3. Base requirements and thickness depend on highest possible fall. Consult manufacturer for base type—sand, rubber tiles, poured-in-place rubber.
☐	☐	☐	4. All finishes are powder coated (specify colors).
☐	☐	☐	5. No exposed bolts, nuts, or sharp edges.
☐	☐	☐	6. Model number correctly specified and availability confirmed with supplier.
☐	☐	☐	7. Anchoring and mounting details per manufacturer specifications.
☐	☐	☐	8. Limit use of metal/aluminum slides in hot climates.
☐	☐	☐	9. Provide adult supervision area with shade covering.

Recorded by: _____ Date: _____

Approved by: _____ Date: _____

CHECKLIST 35   SPECIALTY ITEMS: ROOFTOP GARDENS

Project: _____

Date: _____ Project # _____

Y	N	NA	
☐	☐	☐	1. Determine budget allocation and design responsibility between landscape architect and architect. Waterproofing, protection board, and screed typically under architect's scope. Detailing and specifications coordinated.
☐	☐	☐	2. Planting depth requirements:
☐	☐	☐	a. lawn/groundcover—12 inches soil + 6 inches drainage layer
☐	☐	☐	b. shrubs—24 inches soil + 6 inches drainage layer
☐	☐	☐	c. specimen shrubs/small trees—36 inches soil + 6 inches drainage layer
☐	☐	☐	d. large trees—48 inches soil + 6 inches drainage layer
☐	☐	☐	3. Indicate areas of lightweight fill polystyrene foam (3 lb./c.f.).
☐	☐	☐	4. Coordinate and show locations of water and electrical lines including irrigation, lighting, and drainage sleeves.
☐	☐	☐	5. Coordinate weight allowances for paving, planting, and water features with structural engineer.
☐	☐	☐	6. System design coordinated and detailed. Paving design using pedestals or direct installation to deck. Planting using gravel or drainage carton system.
☐	☐	☐	7. Waterproofing type for planter walls indicating either fluid applied or membrane system.
☐	☐	☐	8. Coordinate height of parapet walls with architect. Verify handrail height meets codes.
☐	☐	☐	9. Allow paving or gravel apron 18 inches wide at all building faces for drainage and window washing equipment.
☐	☐	☐	10. Coordinate roof drainage pipes and impact to the landscape design with architect.
☐	☐	☐	11. Coordinate water feature requirements to rooftop with architect and engineer.
☐	☐	☐	12. Coordinate all piping and sleeves for irrigation, drainage, lighting, and water features.

Recorded by: _____ Date: _____

Approved by: _____ Date: _____

CHECKLIST 36   SPECIALTY ITEMS: WOOD DECKS AND TRELLISES

Project: _____

Date: _____ Project # _____

DESIGN ISSUES

Y	N	NA	
☐	☐	☐	1. Review all framing plan connections, posts, beams, joists, and footings with structural engineer.
☐	☐	☐	2. Check and verify design loads.
☐	☐	☐	3. Heights of deck, railings, and fences conform to local codes.
☐	☐	☐	4. Indicate drainage under deck.
☐	☐	☐	5. Coordinate threshold connections with architect.
☐	☐	☐	6. Allow maximum 1/8 inch (3 mm) space between planks.
☐	☐	☐	7. Note planks are to be laid bark side up.
☐	☐	☐	8. No wood to contact soil.
☐	☐	☐	9. Concrete for post footings is at least 2 inches below frost line.

WOOD

Y	N	NA	
☐	☐	☐	1. Specify type of wood, grade, and treatment.
☐	☐	☐	2. Specify wood finish—stain, paint, sealant, preservatives.
☐	☐	☐	3. No wood to contact soil unless treated with penta/creosote.
☐	☐	☐	4. Note different structural strengths of wood types. Refer to tables for proper spacing.

HARDWARE

Y	N	NA	
☐	☐	☐	1. Specify all hardware and nails to be hot dipped galvanized.
☐	☐	☐	2. Specify exposed hardware color and finish.
☐	☐	☐	3. Indicate plank nailing design.

☐ ☐ ☐   4. Specify finish nails or screws for planking.

☐ ☐ ☐   5. Do not allow exposed bolt threads in pedestrian walkway areas.

☐ ☐ ☐   6. Specify that hammer-damaged planks are to be replaced.

Recorded by: _____   Date: _____

Approved by: _____   Date: _____

CHECKLIST 37   SPECIALTY ITEMS: RETAINING WALLS

Project: _____

Date: _____ Project # _____

WALL STRUCTURE

Y	N	NA	
☐	☐	☐	1. Type of walls:
☐	☐	☐	a. Embankments—turf, rip-rap, mesh, concrete, stone, brick. Maximum 1.5:1 slope.
☐	☐	☐	b. Stack walls—dry, gabions, crib, pre-cast block.
☐	☐	☐	c. Rigid walls—gravity, cantilevered, counter fort.
☐	☐	☐	2. Review with structural and soils engineers—soil weight, bearing capacity, friction coefficient, moisture content, frost, seismic considerations, surcharge.
☐	☐	☐	3. Indicate vertical expansion joints.
☐	☐	☐	4. Indicate wall material (concrete, masonry, dry or mortared stone, railroad ties/wood, concrete block, metal bin).
☐	☐	☐	5. Show reinforcement.
☐	☐	☐	6. Minimum 12 inches soil fill over top of footings in planting areas.
☐	☐	☐	7. Show degree of wall batter.
☐	☐	☐	8. Walls over 48 inches require a structural engineer design.
☐	☐	☐	9. Height, setback, and material conform to local codes.
☐	☐	☐	10. Footing depth is at least 2 inches below frost line.

DRAINAGE

Y	N	NA	
☐	☐	☐	1. Weepholes shown typically at 1-1/2 inches PVC @ 3–10 feet O.C.
☐	☐	☐	2. Drainage at back of wall shown. Continuous back drain with perforated pipe and tie into drainage system.
☐	☐	☐	3. Swale at top of wall to intercept overflow.
☐	☐	☐	4. Minimize surcharges on wall. Review with structural engineer.
☐	☐	☐	5. Wall caps slope to drain and overhangs have drips below.

FINISH

Y	N	NA	
☐	☐	☐	1. Indicate material of wall.
☐	☐	☐	2. Specify applied finish (GFRC, form-liners, mesh with plants, gabions, shotcrete, gunite, plaster, tile, wood, exposed aggregate).
☐	☐	☐	3. Prefabricated systems and interlocking blocks—specify manufacturer, model number, and color.
☐	☐	☐	4. Mortar type, design, color, and grout.
☐	☐	☐	5. Wall cap detail and dimensioning.

Recorded by: _____ Date: _____

Approved by: _____ Date: _____

CHECKLIST 38   SPECIALTY ITEMS: STREETS AND PARKING

Project: _____

Date: _____ Project # _____

STREET DESIGN CRITERIA/CONSIDERATIONS

Y	N	NA	
☐	☐	☐	1. Road classifications
☐	☐	☐	2. Right of way
☐	☐	☐	3. Sight distances
☐	☐	☐	4. Design speed
☐	☐	☐	5. Widths
☐	☐	☐	6. Horizontal alignment
☐	☐	☐	7. Vertical alignment
☐	☐	☐	8. Utility coordination—water, sewer, storm drain, telephone, cable TV, poles, electric, manholes, hydrants, signals, utility boxes, gas lines
☐	☐	☐	9. Signage/billboards
☐	☐	☐	10. Lighting
☐	☐	☐	11. Intersections—visibility triangles/radii
☐	☐	☐	12. Driveways
☐	☐	☐	13. Sidewalks/pedestrian crossings
☐	☐	☐	14. Street trees
☐	☐	☐	15. Drainage
☐	☐	☐	16. Fire lanes
☐	☐	☐	17. Service access
☐	☐	☐	18. Culs-de-sac—length
☐	☐	☐	19. Parking garage structure and circulation

PARKING DESIGN CRITERIA/CONSIDERATIONS

Y	N	NA	
☐	☐	☐	1. Spaces required
☐	☐	☐	2. Accessibility spaces required
☐	☐	☐	3. Runoff drainage mitigated

☐ ☐ ☐   4. Paving material

☐ ☐ ☐   5. Bay design/orientation

☐ ☐ ☐   6. Pedestrian circulation patterns

☐ ☐ ☐   7. Shade trees

☐ ☐ ☐   8. Lighting

Recorded by: _____   Date: _____

Approved by: _____   Date: _____

CHECKLIST 39   SPECIFICATIONS CHECKLIST

Project: _____

Date: _____ Project # _____

BID DOCUMENTS

Y	N	NA	
☐	☐	☐	1. Format per client/agency requirements.
☐	☐	☐	2. If landscape portion of work is a subcontract under the main contract, obtain bid documents, contract forms, and general conditions from client, quantity surveyor, or architect.
☐	☐	☐	3. If landscape work is under a government contract, obtain bid documents from the agency governing the work.
☐	☐	☐	4. Bid documents to include:
☐	☐	☐	a. cover page/table of contents
☐	☐	☐	b. invitation to bid
☐	☐	☐	c. instruction to bidders
☐	☐	☐	d. bid form—lump sum/unit price schedules
☐	☐	☐	e. bid bond
☐	☐	☐	5. Bid/tender deposit required by owner

CONTRACT FORMS

Y	N	NA	
☐	☐	☐	1. Agreement form
☐	☐	☐	2. Proof of insurance form
☐	☐	☐	3. Performance bond
☐	☐	☐	4. Labor and materials bond
☐	☐	☐	5. Payment bond
☐	☐	☐	6. Surety bond
☐	☐	☐	7. Maintenance bond
☐	☐	☐	8. Supplementary conditions (usually federal projects only)

CONTRACT GENERAL CONDITIONS

Y   N   NA

☐   ☐   ☐   1. Select appropriate conditions of the contract:

☐   ☐   ☐   a. AIA Document A201

☐   ☐   ☐   b. ASLA Conditions of the Contract

☐   ☐   ☐   c. CSI Conditions of the Contract

SPECIFICATIONS

Y   N   NA

☐   ☐   ☐   1. List of drawings and details.

☐   ☐   ☐   2. Format according to CSI MasterFormat—16 Divisions.

☐   ☐   ☐   3. Review selection of Division 1—General Requirements with owner.

☐   ☐   ☐   4. List of suppliers/equipment references.

☐   ☐   ☐   5. Review scope of work to ensure all areas are covered by specifications.

☐   ☐   ☐   6. Incorporate consultants' sections.

☐   ☐   ☐   7. Incorporate manufacturers' specifications.

☐   ☐   ☐   8. Define who prepares operations and maintenance manuals.

☐   ☐   ☐   9. Define who prepares record drawings.

☐   ☐   ☐   10. Shop drawing submittal requirements.

☐   ☐   ☐   11. Latest codes and standards referenced.

☐   ☐   ☐   12. Clause for owner approval of subcontractors.

☐   ☐   ☐   13. Sample and submission criteria.

☐   ☐   ☐   14. Verify cross-referenced sections are included.

☐   ☐   ☐   15. Include bid alternates, if any.

☐   ☐   ☐   16. Include clause that if drawings and specifications conflict, specifications prevail.

☐   ☐   ☐   17. Reference to city/local codes, if applicable.

BILL OF QUANTITIES

Y	N	NA	
☐	☐	☐	1. Determine if itemized (measurement) contract or lump sum contract.
☐	☐	☐	2. Bill No. 1—General Conditions/Preliminaries.
☐	☐	☐	3. Bill No. 2—Prime Cost/Provisional Sums.
☐	☐	☐	4. Bill No. 3—Bill of Quantities.
☐	☐	☐	5. Unit rate schedule.

VERIFICATION

Y	N	NA	
☐	☐	☐	1. Distribute to owner and relevant consultants for review and comment.
☐	☐	☐	2. Complete, sign, and file checklist.
☐	☐	☐	3. Place landscape architect seal.

Recorded by: _____   Date: _____

Approved by: _____   Date: _____

CHECKLIST 40   COST ESTIMATE CHECKLIST

Project: _____

Date: _____ Project # _____

Y	N	NA	
☐	☐	☐	1. Format follows CSI MasterFormat—16 Divisions.
☐	☐	☐	2. All cost estimates have a standard clause indicating that the costs reflected are an opinion of probable costs prepared under reasonable care but are not guaranteed, as the landscape architect has no control over labor, materials, and equipment costs or contractor competitive bidding.
☐	☐	☐	3. Indicate phase of work covered by the estimate (conceptual, design development, construction).
☐	☐	☐	4. Include contingency sum.
☐	☐	☐	5. Prices from suppliers include normal labor and installation costs.
☐	☐	☐	6. Include consultant estimated costs.
☐	☐	☐	7. Categorize estimate by quantity and unit cost.
☐	☐	☐	8. Final cost estimate (construction) based on the bill of quantities.
☐	☐	☐	9. Estimate to be reviewed and approved by client before proceeding to next phase of work.
			10. Cost figures taken from:
☐	☐	☐	a. Previous company project
☐	☐	☐	b. Cost data file
☐	☐	☐	c. Cost data book _____
☐	☐	☐	d. Contractor pre-bid _____
☐	☐	☐	e. Other _____
☐	☐	☐	11. Quantities double-checked for construction documents.
☐	☐	☐	12. Unit rates set per project scale (smaller projects have higher unit rates).
☐	☐	☐	13. Inflation contingency for large-scale project
☐	☐	☐	14. Verify CAD generated quantities on a hard copy print.

Recorded by: _____ Date: _____

Approved by: _____ Date: _____

CHECKLIST 41   BIDDING/TENDER CHECKLIST

Project: _____

Date: _____ Project # _____

PREPARATION FOR BID

Y	N	NA	
☐	☐	☐	1. Verify documents to include in bid set:
☐	☐	☐	a. plans
☐	☐	☐	b. specifications
☐	☐	☐	c. bid documents (if separate from specifications)
☐	☐	☐	d. number of copies required
☐	☐	☐	2. Consult with client and/or agency on bid process and time allotted.
☐	☐	☐	3. Prepare advertisements.
☐	☐	☐	4. Check that client has allowed contingency sum for future change orders.
☐	☐	☐	5. Type of bidding:
☐	☐	☐	a. competitive
☐	☐	☐	b. direct selection by owner
☐	☐	☐	c. design/build
☐	☐	☐	d. private
☐	☐	☐	e. public

INVITATION TO BID

Y	N	NA	
☐	☐	☐	1. Establish prequalified bidder list for private tenders.
☐	☐	☐	2. For public tenders, obtain necessary invitation and instruction to bidder forms and procedures from agency in charge.
☐	☐	☐	3. Print required number of bid sets and sequentially number and date each set. Stamp for bidding purposes only.
☐	☐	☐	4. Record collection and return of each set. Collect tender deposit for documents if required.

BID PROCESS

Y	N	NA	
☐	☐	☐	1. Attend pre-bid meeting.
☐	☐	☐	2. Answer all bid queries in writing and copy to all bidders. Include bidder's questions and answers.
☐	☐	☐	3. Prepare necessary addendums.

BID ANALYSIS

Y	N	NA	
☐	☐	☐	1. Coordinate with clients' quantity surveyor regarding any contract queries.
☐	☐	☐	2. Assist client in analyzing bids.
☐	☐	☐	3. Determine statistical mean of all bids.
☐	☐	☐	4. Check that bid form is signed.
☐	☐	☐	5. Check for errors in computing.
☐	☐	☐	6. Confirm contractor certificates of insurance.
☐	☐	☐	7. Check all line items are completed.
☐	☐	☐	8. Check for contractor exceptions, stipulations, or qualifications to the bid.
☐	☐	☐	9. Prepare tender report and recommendation to client.
☐	☐	☐	10. Assist client in contract and award.
☐	☐	☐	11. Update cost data file with latest unit rates.

AWARD

Y	N	NA	
☐	☐	☐	1. Letter of intent from owner to contractor.
☐	☐	☐	2. Contract between owner/contractor signed.
☐	☐	☐	3. All certificates of insurance and bonds obtained.
☐	☐	☐	4. Notice for contractor to proceed.

Recorded by: _____   Date: _____

Approved by: _____   Date: _____

CHECKLIST 42   SITE OBSERVATION CHECKLIST

Project: _____

Date: _____ Project # _____

PROJECT START-UP

Y   N   NA

☐ ☐ ☐   1. Attend pre-construction meeting with client, consultants, contractor, subcontractors, and agencies.

☐ ☐ ☐   2. Establish flow of communication and persons in charge during construction period.

☐ ☐ ☐   3. Contractor to establish a project schedule with critical milestones and dates. This should allow contingencies for overruns due to construction methods and weather. Review with client.

☐ ☐ ☐   4. Appoint internal manpower responsibilities, tasks, and time budget.

☐ ☐ ☐   5. Review construction documents and specifications with the contractor.

☐ ☐ ☐   6. Contractor to list and obtain any permits required during the course of the work.

☐ ☐ ☐   7. Establish shop drawing and submittal log with dates and process for submission and approvals.

☐ ☐ ☐   8. Provide contractor a list of mockup samples to be done.

☐ ☐ ☐   9. Establish photographic record schedule. Take initial site photos.

☐ ☐ ☐   10. Contractor and landscape architect to develop a chart of events and critical milestones during construction when site visits by landscape architect will be necessary.

☐ ☐ ☐   11. Establish a process for reviewing change orders and RFIs.

☐ ☐ ☐   12. Contractor to submit construction cost estimate breakdown.

☐ ☐ ☐   13. Contractor to submit site plan for location of job trailer, material storage on site, rest rooms, access routes on site, parking, trash areas, and field sample area.

☐ ☐ ☐   14. Contractor to appoint safety officer. First aid procedures posted and OSHA safety logs to be reviewed.

☐ ☐ ☐   15. Certificates of compliance to be obtained before ordering and delivery of materials.

☐ ☐ ☐   16. Start project file for construction phase of work. Make reduced set of drawings.

☐ ☐ ☐   17. Contractor to submit procedures for site rules, regulations, and security.

☐ ☐ ☐ 18. Review methods and procedures for progress payments with the owner and contractor.

☐ ☐ ☐ 19. Discuss subcontractor approval procedures .

☐ ☐ ☐ 20. Establish a time limit for contractor to identify discrepancies in drawings between consultants.

DEMOLITION

Y   **N**   **NA**

☐ ☐ ☐ 1. Existing items to remain identified and protected.

☐ ☐ ☐ 2. Trees tagged for removal.

☐ ☐ ☐ 3. Existing trees protected from grading.

☐ ☐ ☐ 4. Construction of site hoarding.

☐ ☐ ☐ 5. Site clearing and grubbing completed.

☐ ☐ ☐ 6. Underground utilities clearly marked.

☐ ☐ ☐ 7. Construction limits of work identified.

☐ ☐ ☐ 8. Topsoil stripping and stockpiling.

☐ ☐ ☐ 9. Rock removal.

GRADING

Y   **N**   **NA**

☐ ☐ ☐ 1. Rough grading completed.

☐ ☐ ☐ 2. Layout of catch basins, deck drains, inlets, and outlets per plan.

☐ ☐ ☐ 3. Perforated pipes and drain lines per plan.

☐ ☐ ☐ 4. Sleeves installed under paving for drainage, irrigation, and electrical lighting uses.

☐ ☐ ☐ 5. Drain lines and weep-holes protected from fill during construction.

☐ ☐ ☐ 6. Sufficient soil cover over underground pipes.

☐ ☐ ☐ 7. Planter box drains installed.

☐ ☐ ☐ 8. Fountain and pool drains installed.

☐ ☐ ☐ 9. Check waterproofing for punctures and correct overlapping.

☐ ☐ ☐ 10. Fine grading completed.

☐ ☐ ☐ 11. Water test for positive flow on all paved surfaces.

☐	☐	☐	12. Water test all drainage pipes to ensure positive flow.
☐	☐	☐	13. Verification of excavations and footing subgrades.
☐	☐	☐	14. Test reports provided by contractor:
☐	☐	☐	a. compressive strength of soil strata
☐	☐	☐	b. soil compaction prior to concrete pouring
☐	☐	☐	c. import fill material
☐	☐	☐	15. Base fill material records and sieve analysis.

CONSTRUCTION

Y	N	NA	
☐	☐	☐	1. Layout of all construction items reviewed prior to installation.
☐	☐	☐	2. Concrete forms checked prior to pouring. Reinforcement free of rust.
☐	☐	☐	3. Wall footings and reinforcement checked and verified by engineer.
☐	☐	☐	4. Compaction specifications and engineer requirements.
☐	☐	☐	5. Concrete slump tests performed and recorded.
☐	☐	☐	6. Material types, textures, and colors conform to approved samples.
☐	☐	☐	7. Expansion and control joints installed per plans.
☐	☐	☐	8. Furnishings installed per manufacturer specifications.
☐	☐	☐	9. Walls and fences meet code requirements.
☐	☐	☐	10. Verify accessible routes.
☐	☐	☐	11. Underground utilities clearly marked until construction completion.
☐	☐	☐	12. Wood kept dry during construction.
☐	☐	☐	13. Welding tests performed and recorded.
☐	☐	☐	14. Testing and commissioning of pools, fountains, and water features completed and documented.
☐	☐	☐	15. Waterproofing checked by manufacturer to facilitate warranty.
☐	☐	☐	16. Plaster, paint, and stain samples approved.

IRRIGATION

Y	N	NA	
☐	☐	☐	1. Separate sleeves installed for electrical and water supply.
☐	☐	☐	2. Head locations and type per plans.

☐ ☐ ☐   3. Meter and backflow preventer installed per code requirements.

☐ ☐ ☐   4. Pressure regulator/reducer installed.

☐ ☐ ☐   5. Hose bibs and quick couplers installed per plans.

☐ ☐ ☐   6. Pumps/filters installed per plans.

☐ ☐ ☐   7. Gate valves installed per plans.

☐ ☐ ☐   8. Controller installed and programmed.

☐ ☐ ☐   9. Head adjustment and coverage tests performed for all areas.

☐ ☐ ☐   10. No irrigation overspill on walkways and roads.

☐ ☐ ☐   11. Testing and commissioning completed and documented.

☐ ☐ ☐   12. Maintenance and operating manual submitted by contractor.

LIGHTING

Y   N   NA

☐ ☐ ☐   1. Fixture type, lamps, and wattage conforms to plans.

☐ ☐ ☐   2. Pole and bollard setting out approved prior to installation.

☐ ☐ ☐   3. Electrical sleeves separate from drainage and irrigation sleeves.

☐ ☐ ☐   4. Fixture installation conforms to details.

☐ ☐ ☐   5. Buried wires flagged during construction.

☐ ☐ ☐   6. Nighttime adjustment of fixture angles completed.

☐ ☐ ☐   7. Testing and commissioning completed and documented.

PLANTING

Y   N   NA

☐ ☐ ☐   1. Visit nurseries to tag specimen trees and plant material.

☐ ☐ ☐   2. Tree staking approved prior to installation.

☐ ☐ ☐   3. Bed setting out approved prior to installation. Verify sun and shade conditions in beds prior to planting.

☐ ☐ ☐   4. Fine grading approved.

☐ ☐ ☐   5. Soil preparation to specifications. Retest for verification. Planting beds to be free of debris before backfill.

☐ ☐ ☐   6. Quantity and size of plant material conforms to plans.

☐ ☐ ☐   7. Condition of plant material conforms to specifications.

☐ ☐ ☐   8. Pottery and hanging baskets per plans.

☐ ☐ ☐   9. Trees next to pavement installed with root barriers.

☐ ☐ ☐   10. Trees in lawn areas have trunk guards.

☐ ☐ ☐   11. Sufficient mowing clearance between trees and beds.

☐ ☐ ☐   12. Tree staking completed per details.

☐ ☐ ☐   13. Vine espaliers installed per details.

☐ ☐ ☐   14. Root barriers on trees installed.

FINAL WALKTHROUGH /SUBSTANTIAL COMPLETION

Y   N   NA

☐ ☐ ☐   1. Attend final walkthrough with client, relevant consultants, contractor, subcontractors, and agency representatives. Prepare punch list for outstanding works and defects.

☐ ☐ ☐   2. Review plans, specifications, and checklists to verify all items are completed per design intent.

☐ ☐ ☐   3. Prepare letter of substantial completion as required. Some government/public projects may require AIA Document G704 to be completed.

☐ ☐ ☐   4. Obtain contractor as-built plans and shop drawings for records.

☐ ☐ ☐   5. Obtain operating and maintenance manuals from contractor, including warranties, guarantees, and bonds. Include product information descriptions from manufacturers.

☐ ☐ ☐   6. Certify mechanics' liens paid before release of final payment.

FINAL COMPLETION

Y   N   NA

☐ ☐ ☐   1. Contractor certifies that all suppliers and subcontractors are paid and submits waivers of lien from each.

☐ ☐ ☐   2. All punch list items completed in conformance with contract.

☐ ☐ ☐   3. In states with strict labor laws, payment certificates should be reviewed by an attorney.

☐ ☐ ☐   4. Any surety bond in the contract must receive written approval from the surety company before final payment is made.

☐ ☐ ☐   5. Certificate of compliance issued.

☐ ☐ ☐ 6. Contractor provides maintenance schedule for review.

☐ ☐ ☐ 7. All accounts adjusted and verified.

☐ ☐ ☐ 8. Recommendation to owner for final payment to contractor.

Recorded by: _____ Date: _____

Approved by: _____ Date: _____

CHECKLIST 43   MAINTENANCE CHECKLIST

Project: _____

Date: _____ Project # _____

MAINTENANCE PERIOD START-UP:

Y	N	NA	
☐	☐	☐	1. Review maintenance period schedule with the contractor.
☐	☐	☐	2. Review maintenance manual and task frequency.
☐	☐	☐	3. Review product warranties.

MONTHLY TASK REVIEWS

PLANTING:

Y	N	NA	
☐	☐	☐	1. Watering of plants sufficient.
☐	☐	☐	2. Dead or dying plants replaced.
☐	☐	☐	3. Good condition of plant material. No pests or disease noticed.
☐	☐	☐	4. Lawn areas mowed, edged, and maintained in good condition.
☐	☐	☐	5. Pruning completed as instructed.
☐	☐	☐	6. Weeding and clearing of litter in beds accomplished.
☐	☐	☐	7. Tree staking adjustments made.
☐	☐	☐	8. Annual color change-outs made.
☐	☐	☐	9. Fertilization per specifications and/or maintenance manual. Schedule of fertilization maintained by the contractor.
☐	☐	☐	10. Beds forked and mulched.
☐	☐	☐	11. Bed edging intact.

DRAINAGE:

Y	N	NA	
☐	☐	☐	1. Site checked for ponding/ drainage problems after hard rain.
☐	☐	☐	2. Erosion-damaged areas repaired.
☐	☐	☐	3. Gutters, catch basins, and drainage inlets cleaned of debris.
☐	☐	☐	4. Clean outs and sumps clear.

☐ ☐ ☐   5. Contained planters and pots not waterlogged.

☐ ☐ ☐   6. Slope erosion control fabric intact.

IRRIGATION:

Y   N   NA

☐ ☐ ☐   1. Plant watering is sufficient.

☐ ☐ ☐   2. Conduct watering test to ensure no overspray on walks and driveways.

☐ ☐ ☐   3. Check for damaged irrigation heads.

☐ ☐ ☐   4. Check timer settings.

☐ ☐ ☐   5. Check planter and pot drip systems.

PAVING:

Y   N   NA

☐ ☐ ☐   1. Surface is in good condition with no visible cracks.

☐ ☐ ☐   2. Accessible route clearly marked.

☐ ☐ ☐   3. Manholes and access covers flush with adjacent pavement.

POOLS/FOUNTAINS:

Y   N   NA

☐ ☐ ☐   1. Pumps, equipment, and filters working properly.

☐ ☐ ☐   2. Algae is controlled.

☐ ☐ ☐   3. Containment basins intact with no visible leaking.

☐ ☐ ☐   4. Overflows working properly.

☐ ☐ ☐   5. Pool is clean with proper chemical balance.

☐ ☐ ☐   6. Biological lakes and ponds have healthy fish and plant life.

LIGHTING:

Y   N   NA

☐ ☐ ☐   1. Light fixture adjustments made at night.

☐ ☐ ☐   2. Check for exposed electrical wiring.

☐ ☐ ☐   3. Well lights intact with no water containment.

☐ ☐ ☐   4. Fixtures working properly.

☐ ☐ ☐   5. Signage lighting clear.

MISCELLANEOUS CONSTRUCTION ITEMS:

Y	N	NA	
☐	☐	☐	1. Signage intact and not vandalized.
☐	☐	☐	2. Furnishings properly anchored.
☐	☐	☐	3. Metal work free from rust.
☐	☐	☐	4. Wall surfaces in good condition with no visible cracks.
☐	☐	☐	5. Paint or stain in good condition.
☐	☐	☐	6. Nails, screws, and bolts properly countersunk.

NOTE: A MONTHLY MAINTENANCE OBSERVATION REPORT BASED ON THIS CHECKLIST SHOULD BE PROVIDED TO THE CLIENT AND MAINTENANCE CONTRACTOR.

Recorded by: _____   Date: _____

Approved by: _____   Date: _____

CHECKLIST 44   PROJECT CLOSEOUT

Project: _____

Date: _____ Project # _____

AFTER MAINTENANCE PERIOD ENDS

Y   N   NA

☐   ☐   ☐   1. Send letter to owner at least 15 days prior to the end of the one-year maintenance period reminding of handover.

☐   ☐   ☐   2. Conduct final site walkthrough with owner and maintenance contractor for final handover.

☐   ☐   ☐   3. Photograph drawings and project site for future marketing.

☐   ☐   ☐   4. Review details to be incorporated into standards file.

☐   ☐   ☐   5. Send backups of word processing and CAD disks to off-site storage area.

☐   ☐   ☐   6. Roll and file all drawings in tube and label. Store in dead file.

☐   ☐   ☐   7. File specification booklets in box, label, and store in dead file.

☐   ☐   ☐   8. Complete Project Evaluation Checklist and review with principal in charge.

Recorded by: _____ Date: _____

Approved by: _____ Date: _____

CHECKLIST 45   CLIENT EVALUATION FORM

Project: _____

Date: _____

E = Excellent

S = Satisfactory

N = Needs Improvement

P = Problem Area

E	S	N	P	
☐	☐	☐	☐	1. Were your goals and expectations for the project met?
☐	☐	☐	☐	2. Was there a strong design concept?
☐	☐	☐	☐	3. Was the project schedule met?
☐	☐	☐	☐	4. Was the project in budget?
☐	☐	☐	☐	5. Was the project team communication effective?
☐	☐	☐	☐	6. Were the drawings delivered on time?
☐	☐	☐	☐	7. How was the drawing quality and completeness?
☐	☐	☐	☐	8. Was the design fee cost compatable to services provided?
☐	☐	☐	☐	OVERALL RATING

Comments on positive areas of performance:

_____

_____

_____

_____

Comments on negative areas of performance:

_____

_____

_____

_____

Would you use us again on future projects? Why?

_____

_____

_____

_____

CHECKLIST 46   PROJECT EVALUATION CHECKLIST

Project: _____

Date: _____ Project # _____

NOTE: A DETAILED WRITTEN CLARIFICATION SHOULD BE MADE PERTAINING TO ANY ITEMS IDENTIFIED AS 'NO' ON THIS CHECKLIST.

PROJECT ISSUES

Y	N	NA	
☐	☐	☐	1. Did the project meet the clients' goals and expectations?
☐	☐	☐	2. Did the project meet the teams' goals and expectations?
☐	☐	☐	3. Was the design concept successfully translated into built form?
☐	☐	☐	4. Was the design quality of the project maintained as planned?
☐	☐	☐	5. Were the plans and specifications free from errors or omissions?
☐	☐	☐	6. Is this a project that can be used for marketing?
☐	☐	☐	7. Is this project a candidate for awards submission?
☐	☐	☐	8. Is this a type of project that has been done in the past?
☐	☐	☐	9. Were the code requirements easily fulfilled?
☐	☐	☐	10. Was the design easy to construct?

PROJECT TEAM/MANAGEMENT ISSUES

Y	N	NA	
☐	☐	☐	1. Did the work schedule flow smoothly?
☐	☐	☐	2. Was good communication maintained between project team members?
☐	☐	☐	3. Did the management and staff work together effectively?

BUDGET ISSUES

Y	N	NA	
☐	☐	☐	1. Was the project completed within budget?
☐	☐	☐	2. Was the budget sufficient for this type of project?
☐	☐	☐	3. Were deadlines met without overtime?
☐	☐	☐	4. Were project expenses controlled?
☐	☐	☐	5. Were the final costs in line with the work plan projections?
☐	☐	☐	6. Did the design meet the client's budget?

SCHEDULING ISSUES

Y	N	NA	
☐	☐	☐	1. Was the project schedule met?
☐	☐	☐	2. Was the schedule reasonable?
☐	☐	☐	3. Was the schedule under control during the project?
☐	☐	☐	4. Was the project within reasonable proximity to the office?
☐	☐	☐	5. Was the schedule maintained even with unexpected contingencies?

CLIENT ISSUES

Y	N	NA	
☐	☐	☐	1. Have we worked with the client on past projects?
☐	☐	☐	2. Was positive communication with the client maintained?
☐	☐	☐	3. Was the client satisfied with the results and our performance?
☐	☐	☐	4. Will the client hire us in the future?
☐	☐	☐	5. Did the client fulfill promised obligations to us (e.g., data collection, base information, approvals)?
☐	☐	☐	6. Was invoicing issued promptly?
☐	☐	☐	7. Was client payment on time?

CONSULTANT/CONTRACTOR ISSUES

Y	N	NA	
☐	☐	☐	1. Was positive communication maintained with the clients' consultants and contractor?
☐	☐	☐	2. Was the other consultants' performance satisfactory?
☐	☐	☐	3. Was the contractor qualified to perform the work?
☐	☐	☐	4. Was the work installed properly according to the plans and specifications?
☐	☐	☐	5. Was the contractor easy to work with?
☐	☐	☐	6. Should the contractor be retained on our prequalified bidders list?

Recorded by: _____ Date: _____

Approved by: _____ Date: _____

Bibliography

Part I

Books and Manuscripts

American Society of Landscape Architects. *Landscape Architects Handbook of Professional Practice*. ASLA, 1972.

Laurie, Michael. *An Introduction to Landscape Architecture*. New York: Elsevier Science Publishing Co., Inc., 1975.

Marshall, Lane. *Landscape Architecture: Guidelines to Professional Practice*. Washington, D.C.: ASLA, 1981.

Newton, Norman. *Design on the Land*. Cambridge, Mass.: Belknap Press of Harvard University, 1971.

Rogers, Elizabeth Barlow. *Landscape Design: A Cultural and Architectural History*. New York: Harry N. Abrams, 2001.

Rogers, Walter. *The Professional Practice of Landscape Architecture*. New York: John Wiley and Sons, 1997.

Schatz, Alex P. *Regulation of Landscape Architecture and the Protection of Public Health, Safety and Welfare*. Produced for ASLA, Washington, D.C., October, 2003.

Sharky, Bruce. *Ready, Set, Practice: Elements of Landscape Architecture Professional Practice*. New York: John Wiley and Sons, 1994.

Texas Board of Architectural Examiners. *Rules and Regulations of the Board Regulating the Practice of Landscape Architecture*. 2003. Also available online at http://www.tbae.state.tx.us.

URLs (Uniform Resource Locators)

American Society of Landscape Architects. "ASLA Code of Professional Ethics." *Leaders Handbook* (2001). From: http://www.asla.org/governance/ldrshdbk/code.htm.

American Society of Landscape Architects. *The Practice of Landscape Architecture: Cases Impacting the Public's Health, Safety, and Welfare* (May 2002). From: http://www.asla.org/members/govtaffairs/licensure/pdf/phsw-final.pdf.

American Society of Landscape Architects. "What is Landscape Architecture?" (2001). From: http://www.asla.org/nonmembers/publicrelations/What_is_ASLA.cfm.

PART II

Books and Manuscripts

Bennett, Bruce, Brenda Bryant, Gary VandenBos, and Addison Greenwood. *Professional Liability and Risk Management.* Washington, D.C: American Psychological Association, 1990.

Cushman, Robert F. *Avoiding Liability in Architecture, Design and Construction.* New York: John Wiley and Sons, 1983.

Greenstreet, Bob, and Karen Greenstreet. *The Architect's Guide to Law and Practice.* New York: Van Nostrand Reinhold, 1984.

Holland, Kent. *Architectural/Engineering Contracts: Risk Management Guide.* New York: Zurich Insurance, 1997/1998.

Hungelmann, Jack. *Insurance for Dummies.* New York: Hungry Minds, 2001.

Merritt, Frederick S., and Jonathon T. Ricketts. *Building Design and Construction Handbook.* 6th ed. Philippines: McGraw-Hill Education (Asia), 2001.

Rogers, Walter. *The Professional Practice of Landscape Architecture.* New York: John Wiley and Sons, 1997.

Schatz, Alex P. *Regulation of Landscape Architecture and the Protection of Public Health, Safety and Welfare.* Produced for ASLA, Washington, D.C., October, 2003.

Streeter, Harrison. *Professional Liability of Architects and Engineers.* New York: John Wiley and Sons, 1988.

URLs (Uniform Resource Locators)

American Society of Landscape Architects. *The Practice of Landscape Architecture: Cases Impacting the Public's Health, Safety, and Welfare* (May 2002) From: http://www.asla.org/members/govtaffairs/licensure/pdf/phsw-final.pdf.

Leatzow, Jim. "Managing Risks to Avoid Being Sued: Basic Training for Smaller Landscape Architectural Firms" (March 8, 2001). From: http://www.asla.org/nonmembers/education/archive.htm.

Marinelli, Dominic. "Applying State and Federal Accessibility Standards" (2002). From: http://gateway.ilearning.com/c2ed/.

Saucerman, S.S. "An Alternative to Litigation," *Plumbing and Mechanical Magazine* (September 28, 2000). From: http://www.pmmag.com/pm/cda/articleinformation/features/bnp_features_item/011572,00+en-uss_01dbc.html.

PART III

Books and Manuscripts

Burnstein, David, and Frank A. Stasiowski. *Project Management for the Design Professional.* New York: John Wiley and Sons, 1982.

Dines, Nicholas, and Kyle Brown. *Landscape Architect's Portable Handbook.* New York: McGraw-Hill, 2001.

Goetsch, David. *Total Quality Handbook.* New Jersey: Prentice-Hall, 2001.

Goetsch, David, and Stanley Davis. *Understanding and Implementing ISO 9000:2000.* 2nd ed. New Jersey: Prentice-Hall, 2002.

Hoyle, David. *ISO 9000:2000: An A-Z Guide.* Oxford: Butterworth-Heinemann, 2003.

Merritt, Frederick S., and Jonathon T. Ricketts. *Building Design and Construction Handbook.* 6th ed. Philippines: McGraw-Hill Education (Asia), 2001.

Stasiowski, Frank A., and David Burstein. *Total Quality Project Management for the Design Firm.* New York: John Wiley and Sons, 1994.

Sulzinger, Richard, and Robert Clements. *Marketing Design Services: Principles, Management, and Strategies for Landscape Architecture Practices.* Washington, D.C.: Professional Practice Institute of ASLA, 1983.

URLs (Uniform Resource Locators)

Sipes, James L. "Improving Productivity, Efficiency, and Quality of CADD Drawings" (April 19, 2001). From: http://www.asla.org/nonmembers/education/archive.htm.

PART IV

Books and Manuscripts

Americans with Disabilities Act. *Americans with Disability Act Handbook.* Appendix B: ADA Accessibility Guidelines. Published by the Equal Opportunity Commission and the U.S. Department of Justice, October 1991.

Carpenter, Jot. *Handbook of Landscape Architectural Construction.* Landscape Architecture Foundation, 1976.

Construction Specification Institute. *Masterformat— Master List of Section Titles and Numbers.* Washington, D.C.: Construction Specifications Institute, 1981.

DeChiara, Joseph, and Lee Koppelman. *Urban Planning and Design Criteria.* 2nd ed. New York: Van Nostrand Reinhold, 1975.

Department of Justice. "28 CFR Part 36: ADA Standards for Accessible Design," in *Code of Federal Regulations.* 1994. Also available online at http://www.usdoj.gov/crt/ada/stdspdf.htm.

Dines, Nicholas, and Kyle Brown. *Landscape Architect's Portable Handbook.* New York: McGraw-Hill, 2001.

Dines, Nicholas, and Charles Harris. *Time Saver Standards for Landscape Architecture,* 2nd ed. New York: McGraw-Hill, 1997.

Falero, Eugenio, and Santiago Alonzo. *Quantitative Techniques in Landscape Planning.* Florida: CRC Press, 1995.

LaGro Jr., James A. *Site Analysis.* New York: John Wiley and Sons, 2001.

Lynch, Kevin. *The Image of the City.* Cambridge: MIT Press, 1960.

McHarg, Ian. *Design with Nature.* New York: Doubleday/National History Press, 1969.

Merritt, Frederick S., and Jonathon T. Ricketts. *Building Design and Construction Handbook.* 6th ed. Philippines: McGraw-Hill Education (Asia), 2001.

Landphair, Harlow, and Fred Klatt Jr. *Landscape Architectural Construction.* New York: Elsevier, 1979.

Landphair, Harlow, and John Motloch. *Site Reconnaissance and Engineering: An Introduction for Architects, Landscape Architects, and Planners.* New York: Elsevier Science, 1985.

Russ, Thomas. *Site Planning and Design Handbook.* New York: McGraw-Hill, 2002.

Simonds, John O. *Landscape Architecture: A Manual of Site Planning and Design.* 3rd ed. New York: McGraw-Hill, 1998.

Strom, Steven, and Kurt Nathan. *Site Engineering for Landscape Architects*, 2nd ed. New York: Van Nostrand Reinhold, 1993.

Walker, Theodore. *Site Design and Construction Detailing*, 3rd ed. New York: Van Nostrand Reinhold, 1992.

Watson, Donald. *Time Saver Standards for Urban Design.* New York: McGraw-Hill, 2003.

URLs (Uniform Resource Locators)

Marinelli, Dominic. "Applying State and Federal Accessibility Standards" (2002). From: http://gateway.ilearning.com/c2ed/.

Terry, Jim. "An Introduction to Universal Design in Exterior Spaces" (2001). From: http://www.gateway.ilearning.com/c2ed/.

U.S. Architectural and Transportation Barriers Compliance Board (Access Board), *Americans with Disabilities Act (ADA), Accessibility Guidelines for Buildings and Facilities.* Appendix A to Part 1191. From: http://www.access-board.gov/adaag/ADAAG.pdf.

INDEX